THE HALF BASEMENT

Written by Boksoon Kim

Preface

My friend Hae Hun Matos stopped by my house. Right before leaving she said to me, "You will write your second book." I responded in my heart, "I don't think so." I faced so many hardships to publish my first book, 'I asked the author' and I did not want to go through that again.

But as time passed, I wanted to write my stories that I wanted to share, but I had not yet spoken. After having lived past 50 years in the mission field, after having watched the lives of those who have lived abroad to serve the Lord, my stories that I want to share have accumulated in me.

The first word that came into my mind was THE HALF BASEMENT even before I began to write a book. Half basement is a synonym of poverty. The rich do not live in the half basement but the poor. Half basement is damp due to moisture coming from the ground. The outside view through the window is not a peaceful greenery but the feet and legs of walking people on the ground. When windows are open to ventilate the air of the half basement, people can easily see the inside of the half basement. Yet the worst will be that one may be trapped inside with no exit at the time of fire or flood. It is not a desirable place to live when one has enough money.

But the Lord led me to a half basement. My life began to sprout, grow, and bloom with flowers in the half basement. My half basement was a place full of love, life, and blessings.

I want to share with missionaries who are now retired my untold stories, the path I had walked.

I want to tell my encouragement and warnings as a guide to the precious servants of the Lord who serve actively in the ministry. I want young people who want to give their lives to serve the Lord to listen to my stories. I pray that the readers of this book may bear abundant fruits in their ministry.

Later I asked Hae Hun why she said to me, "You will write your second book." She answered that she had said that without any specific reason. Her word became irresistible words from the Lord and I wrote this book.

I thank pastor Issac Moon and Mrs. Saeyun Moon for reading and editing my book. I thank Poet Mark Hong who translated my husband's English poem into Korean. I thank pastor Joshua Lee who encouraged me to go on with publication of my books. I thank Chris, Amazon publishing network, Hong, Youngchul, the Korean publisher, and pastor John Lee in Houston CMI church for supporting me with practical help.

Table Of Contents

Chapter 1:
A Miraculous Car Accident

Crash!

I woke up from sleeping from a violent shake like an earthquake. Everything was white, as white as snow. 'Where am I? Am I in heaven?' When I looked around more, I was inside of my car. My car was covered with snow.

I was driving on the Indiana Turnpike toward the Ohio Turnpike. It was cold and snowy. So I was driving slowly at about 60 miles/hour. I fell asleep at the wheel. My car crossed the two yellow midlines, passed the opposite lane, hit a snow pile in the middle of it, and stopped. Because of snow the snow plowing trucks removed snow from the expressways and put the snow into a snow pile. The snow piles were approximately one in every half mile or a quarter mile.

I was alive. My seat belt was intact around me, and I did not have any injury. At that time, in 1975 winter, cars did not have airbags. I was thinking about what to do next. First, I had to get out of the car, and the snow pile sooner the better while I had strength, warm body temperature, and oxygen. Opening the car door was impossible because the snow blocked the door. I could open the window down. The window was manual. But what if the snow falls into the car and makes the inside of the car wet and colder? Suppose that I could get out through the car window, but in which direction should I move without being trapped inside the snow? There were too many uncertainties.

Why not start the engine?

I started the engine and it started!

I put the transmission handle in reverse, slowly and straightly pulled the car out of the snow pile and then the car came out of the snow pile. I crossed the two yellow mid lines and went back to the lane toward Ohio. Later, there was some damage found at the bottom of my car which required repair but it ran until I arrived home safely.

I saw many miracles through this car accident. I was not hurt at all. That was a miracle. It was a miracle that my car hit the snow pile in the middle. Had it hit a couple of yards to the right or to the left, my car might have penetrated through the shallow snow and it might have hit or plunged into the ditch. It was a miracle that my car did not have a head on collision with opposite traffic. The Lord saved my life. I thought that the Lord had something to do with my life and I should not die.

Days ago, before the trip I was invited to a prayer meeting in the church in Chicago. Ever since I left NY, it was the first time that I met the church members. I planned to drive to Chicago, attend the prayer meeting and return back to Toledo that same night. In the morning, I had a test for my German class at the University of Toledo. I did not want to miss the test.

But when I arrived at the church in Chicago, I had to drive another two hours to a place where a prayer meeting was arranged. I drove six hours and I had to drive another two hours. I followed another car. I was exhausted and I started to have double vision. I have poor eyesight and when I am extremely tired, I have double vision. Everything was double, two cars, two lines, two lanes. And I did not know which one was real, and which one was false. I could not tell the car I was following to stop because there was no cell phone at that time.

Anyway, I arrived safely with double visions to a place for a prayer meeting. All the attendants were from the church in Chicago excluding me. Prayer meeting was short with no specific prayer topics and it finished in less than one hour. There were less than a dozen people including me. I still do not understand why they drove two hours to go to pray and drove back two hours. Why didn't they pray at the church building in Chicago?

After the prayer meeting, all drove back to Chicago. On the way back I did not have double vision. Maybe sitting for one hour during the prayer meeting helped me restore my strength. When we returned to Chicago it was very late at night, almost 11 pm. I was ready to go back, and they asked me to stay that night. I insisted that I was leaving. One person said, "Leave her alone. She does whatever she decides to do." Yes, I decided to take the German test in the morning. I would drive six hours and arrive in Toledo early in the morning. I would take some rest and take the examination. But I fell asleep at the wheel and I was driving while sleeping.

After I resumed driving on the Indiana Turnpike toward the Ohio Turnpike, unbelievably I kept on falling asleep again. I pulled my car to the side of the expressway and parked to take a nap. But after I turned off the engine, it was so cold that I could not go to sleep.

When I entered Ohio Turnpike, I was more alert and I made it safely to my attic room. My original plan was to take some rest and go to the class, but instead, I drove to an emergency room because of severe pain in my right leg.

Chapter 2:
Temptation

I was admitted to a hospital. My diagnosis was deep vein thrombosis of my right leg. Less than 24 hours I was driving for almost 18 hours without rest and sleep. My doctor put me on strict bed rest 24/7. I was not allowed to go to the bathroom. I had to use a bedpan. From the toes to groin my right leg was wrapped with two or three electric heating pads with wet towels inside. I was on blood thinner and muscle relaxant. When any blood clot is released into the bloodstream, it would be life threatening. Clot forming process had to be stopped and reversed inside of the vein in my leg.

For several days, I was sleeping in the bed all day long except for meal times. Even though I was sleeping day and night I began to worry about my future. Nursing job requires standing for long hours on foot. I cannot stand long hours any more. I was not sure whether I could work as a nurse at all. If I cannot work as a nurse, how can I support my living in America? How can I pay my rent, car payment, and car insurance next month? Should I go back to Korea to my home town and depend on my family as a sick person? Luckily, I finished my flight payment. I was paying monthly for the one way flight from Korea to NY.

Then a Korean doctor who worked at the same hospital visited me. He was really concerned about my situation. He said to me, "Miss Yun. You need to settle down. My doctor friend just came to Toledo from West Germany. He has not married yet because of studying. He loves studying. When you are discharged from the hospital, I will arrange for you to meet him." Then he left.

I was sleepy. But I knew that it was a temptation. I was once possessed by evil spirits. At that time I learned that evil spirits could come inside my mind and control my feelings and thoughts. The Korean doctor might have thought he was just delivering what he felt good for me and his friend. He would not have realized that the idea was given into his heart and he was just a messenger. After he left I was just amazed how the devil knew my heart exactly. A medical doctor who loves to study and speaks fluent German was an irresistible candidate for marriage. I already liked this doctor from West Germany. I did not have to see him. At the same time, I perceived the spirit of temptation. Temptation is always sweet and hard to overcome.

I had to decide whether I should see this doctor or not. It was a good idea that I settle down with a type of man I like and at the same time solve my financial problem. On the other side, I have God's calling to live to serve God. Can I live a life of calling after I marry this man? Or should I refuse to see this man? Then how can I live with a sick leg? I had to figure it out. But I was very sleepy. I should be awake and have a clear mind to decide about my future.

Why am I so sleepy day and night? Then it dawned on me that I was on sleeping pills to keep me inactive and resting. I

6

did not take sleeping pills but the muscle relaxant had the ingredients of sleeping pills. I had to come out of drowsiness to think right. Then a nurse came and gave me my medicine. I threw them into my mouth and drank half a cup of water as the nurse was watching me. I drank only water but did not swallow the pills. When I put the pills into my mouth, I put them under my tongue. The pills remained under my tongue inside of my mouth. After the nurse left, I spit out the pills in my hand out of my mouth. I removed the muscle relaxant and swallowed the rest. I repeated it again with the next medication. Then I came out of sleepiness. I was alert and had a clear mind.

I sat on my hospital bed and pulled the table over the bed. I opened the Bible Genesis 12:1-3.

The Lord had said to Abram, "Leave your country, your people and your father's household and go to the land I will show you.

"I will make you into a great nation and I will bless you;

I will make your name great, and you will be a blessing.

I will bless those who bless you, and whoever curses you I will curse; and all peoples on earth will be blessed through you."

Genesis 12:1-3

While I was in Korea I prayed to God to send me to a place where He wanted me to go. I would go wherever God sends me. I will live my life as a blessing to others. Whoever meets me will be blessed. This is the life God called me to live. This is the life I chose to live.

The bottom line was; can I continue to live as a blessing even after I marry this doctor? Or will I lose the life of calling if I marry this doctor? There was not an easy answer. My very existence was threatened and I wanted to be safe by marrying this doctor. At the same time, I did not want to lose my life of Genesis 12:1-3. I was searching for an answer to these questions, but unconsciously or subconsciously I had the answer in my mind; marry the doctor and continue to obey God's calling to live as a blessing to others. I just wanted to justify my decision.

But God gave a different answer. As I was thinking this way and that way in my hospital bed, I heard faint sounds from a distance. The sounds were coming closer, closer, a little louder, and louder. I recognized that it was the sounds of prayers of the young brothers and sisters in the church in Korea. After worship services or meetings we prayed for the evangelization of the world with the Gospel according to the command of Jesus. (Acts 1:8) When we prayed, it was loud. When many groups prayed at the same time in a room, the room was filled with loud prayer sounds. That's what I heard in my bed. Then the prayer sounds gradually faded and gone. Brothers and sisters were praying for the world mission. It happened in a very short time like 4 or 5 seconds.

My heart was pierced. I cannot betray them. I cannot betray their prayers for my own well-being. Even if I may lose my job, or lose my leg, I will be faithful to their prayers. I will continue what I have been doing and I will leave everything in the hand of God: job, sick leg, life security, monthly bills, and my future. Let the Lord worry about those of my problems. I will just continue to preach the words.

The answer came from hearing the prayer sounds, not from my reasoning, not from the words of Genesis 12:1-3. The prayer sounds saved one missionary who was going through the temptation. The brothers and sisters might not know that their prayers led one slipping missionary to come back.

"And lead us not into temptation," **Matthew 6:13**

The Lord intervened me to hear the prayer sounds of the brothers and sisters and led me not into temptation.

After 10 days of hospitalization, I was discharged from the hospital at around noon. I did not go to my attic room. From the hospital, I drove to Cleveland for Bible study. I put my still painful right leg on the passenger seat, and I drove with my left leg. Initially I had to be careful of driving with my left leg but soon I was comfortable driving with my left leg.

When I was young, and I don't remember how young I was, I was thinking about using arms. Why do right-handed people use mainly the right hand and not use the left hand? And vice versa; why do left-handed people use mainly the left hand and not use the right hand? I thought that it was in people's thoughts in doing that. My idea was different. Why not use both hands?

I should be able to use both hands. I am right-handed but I will train my left hand and I will use both hands. I began to train my left hand. My parents were worried when they saw me eating with my left hand. They didn't and couldn't stop me from using my left hand because I was a stubborn child. When I was able to do a lot with my left hand except writing, I stopped self-training. I wondered whether this helped me drive with my left leg instantly in time of need.

After missing a test and classes for over 10 days I quit the study of German for good. It would have been a lot better, had I slept a couple of hours in Chicago and had left Chicago at around 3 or 4am. I would have taken the German test at 10am. Then by now I would speak German fluently. That kind of wisdom came to me later in my life after I became older, weaker, and poorer.

I returned to my regular work with the vulnerable right leg. There were times when sharp pain shot in my right leg during work but overall it was getting better. Recovery took a long time. I took blood thinners for a long time. Every day I wore a custom-made elastic panty hose. With a doctor's prescription I went to a business place which made elastic panty hose. One employee measured from toe, both legs, and to waist. It took me time and strength to put this on because it was very tight. I filled the bathtub with warm water and soaked my legs after returning from work. I did not abuse my legs anymore to accomplish my goal. And my right leg was healed completely. Later at work, I saw the Korean doctor who visited me to match me with his friend. He did not say anything about it and I did not say anything.

Chapter 3:
Half Basement

The end of the six months lease of the attic was approaching. It was time for me to move out. When I had time, I walked around University of Toledo and looked for an apartment. I did not save enough money for the security deposit and the first month's rent. Even though I did not have enough money I was moving toward my direction.

My target of evangelism was college students. So I wanted to move near the University of Toledo. There is a saying in Korean, 'If you want to hunt a tiger, go inside of the tiger's den.' I was looking for an apartment near the campus where the majority of tenants were students. I wanted to live among students to teach them the words of God. I came to one such apartment. I opened the door of the main entrance to the inside and entered. On the left side wall there was a bulletin board with many selling and buying advertisements of the tenants.

One advertisement got my attention. It was a sublease advertisement. The apartment was already vacant with 3-4 months remaining lease. Perfect! With less money I could move in. The sublease did not require security deposit. I needed just the remaining rent to move in. The security deposit would be calculated after the end of lease. I contacted the original tenant and moved in with about two weeks rent. The wisdom of God was endless. How could I imagine that I could move into an apartment with two weeks rent? And it was a half basement.

Finally I had my own space. It was a half basement studio apartment, one wide space with a kitchen and a bathroom on one side. The outside ground level was just below the apartment windows and I could see the legs of people walking in the yard. I had no furniture. I had two blankets, some dishes, and cups. Soon I found from the same bulletin an advertisement selling a desk and two chairs. I bought them. The student sellers kindly moved the table to my apartment.

When people have their own spaces, they start to transform the place according to their own taste. I, too, prepared my own space. I prepared my half basement as a place for Bible study. I had a desk and two chairs. Perfect! That's all I needed. At night I spread one blanket over the carpeted floor and covered myself with another blanket. In the morning, I folded them and put them away. When a person came into my half basement, there was no couch, no sofa, no TV, no coffee, and no cookies. There was only one desk, two chairs and the Bible. It meant to be a place just for Bible study. Only those who wanted to study the Bible came in and after the Bible study they had to leave because I did not provide anything besides Bible study.

Half basement is a synonym of poverty. Rich people do not live in a half basement. Poor people live in a half basement. It is damp with humidity from the ground. When I look through the window, I see people's legs instead of nice scenery. When I open the window to ventilate, people can easily peek into the half basement from the ground level. Even worse, people can be trapped with no way out in case of fire or flood. But nothing bothered me.

I was just so thankful that I had my own place to teach the Bible freely. God Himself chose this half basement.

When I lived in a dormitory room back in Seoul, Korea, there was just a desk and a bunker bed in the room. There was not a single picture on the white wall, nor a clock on the wall, nor a plant pot. There was no curtain over the window. There was nothing to please human eyes and minds.

Yet God came to the room three times; to answer my question as the author of the Bible, to baptize me with the Holy Spirit when I confessed my sins, and to answer my protest about preaching the word. The room had no decorations and comfort but had two things; the Bible and my eager heart to learn the meaning of the words and live according to the word. Then God came to the room. That's what I learned and I did the same in my half basement apartment. All I needed was the Bible and sincere hearts seeking God's truth.

One Korean pastor said to me; "Nowadays church building has to be nice. People come to church because of nice buildings." His words are convincing. When church building is completed, church attendants increase. Sure, more people come because the place is nice. But does God come in because of the nice looking building?

Even though my target people were college students, my Bible students were mostly Koreans.

They came to this half basement and studied the Bible with me. One day it was my day off from work. I had four Bible studies that day from morning till night. Before the first Bible study I chose the suitable passages for that person. It took about two hours to prepare and one hour to teach. After the first Bible student left, I began to prepare for the second Bible study. I thought about that person and selected suitable passages for that person. After the second Bible student left, I began to prepare for the third Bible study.

When I finished the fourth Bible study it was at about 10:30pm. It was an intensely long day. I spread one blanket over the carpeted floor and covered myself to go to sleep. Then I had a stomach ache and I couldn't go to sleep. I thought that I had some stomach illness like ulcer. Then I realized that I did not eat anything all day: no breakfast, no lunch, and no dinner. I just forgot to eat. How could that be possible? Yet it happened. I got up and drank some water to calm my stomach. But I did not eat. I was too exhausted to eat.

I put my Korean Bible students in a group and started a group Bible study on Saturdays. As they began to receive the words of God, they said that they wanted to attend Sunday worship service to worship God on Sundays. They said that Bible study on Saturdays was not enough. That meant that they would scatter to other churches to attend Sunday worship services in other churches. I had a different plan with them. I wanted to build a new church to God together with them. Once they scatter to different churches, I cannot gather them together again. So I announced a Sunday worship service in my half basement beginning from the next Sunday.

The Half Basement

foot steps →

Chapter 4:
God Came to the Half Basement

I began to prepare for Sunday worship service. I bought folding chairs. I went to a Christian book store and bought one box of small sized Bibles. There were so many hymn books and I did not know which one to buy. After much consideration I chose one and bought a dozen of them. I made a lectern. I went to a hardware store and bought necessary woods, a hammer, and nails to make a lectern. I had the woods cut in sizes at the hardware store and nailed those woods together at my half basement. It was not as good as the lecterns used in churches but it was good enough for the half basement and good enough to put the Bible and my sermon notes. I bought everything with my own money.

The next Sunday all my Korean Bible students came and we started our first Sunday worship service. We followed the general order of worship service: singing hymns, prayers, and Sunday message, singing hymns, and prayers. I gave the Sunday messages every week. We had no musical instruments like piano or organ. We sang a cappella and I had to sing louder so that others may learn and follow the song. They just listened to the first verse when I sang. They were humming the second verse, and they could sing the third verse together. I myself did not know many songs and we ended up singing the same several songs repeatedly.

After giving a Sunday message I took a day of rest on Monday. On Tuesday I selected passages for next Sunday's message from the whole Bible, from Genesis to Revelation. But sometimes I could not choose my sermon passage until Wednesday and even until Thursday. Then I did not have enough time to prepare the Sunday message. I became uncomfortable, unconfident, and frustrated. This problem continued.

One day I finished my last Bible study late at night. I turned the light off and I spread one blanket in the middle of the room and covered myself with another blanket. I lay on my right side with my face facing the white wall of my apartment. The whole room was very dark. Before I fell asleep, I sensed some brightness in my eyes. So I opened my eyes just a tiny bit to see why I felt some brightness in my eyes in the dark room. I began to open my eyes wider and wider by what I saw.

I saw on the white wall of the room our church people about a dozen of us. The whole room and the wall were dark but the area we appeared was bright. I saw each person and I could tell who each person was. It was like a group picture but real alive, and just heads and upper torsos. Waist down was covered in darkness. And instantly I saw our minds across all of us. Our hearts were greedy for ourselves and stingy to God. I don't remember how this vision faded away or disappeared from the wall.

Our church members were poor. I could never ask them to offer their money to God. It was easier for me to give my money to them. My attitude seemed to be very kind and compassionate. But the sin of stinginess to God was growing among us. In the Bible both the rich and the poor offered to

God. Rich people offered lamb or sheep to God, while the poor offered pigeons. But I did not teach them to offer their pigeons. I was guiding them to keep their pigeons for themselves because they were poor. I was guiding them to keep their money and I will give my money too, because they were poor. The sin of stinginess to God was growing in our church. Unless this problem was corrected, I was leading them to be Christian beggars.

I was not aware of this problem but God came and showed me. I had to overcome my own attitude, human thinking, and I had to teach the poor to offer their money to God within their ability. Offering money to God is offering our hearts to God. I prepared the Sunday message about offering money to God for the first time. A preacher is a messenger. He or she must not add a personal view but must deliver God's message as it is written in the Bible. I had to deliver God's message as it is to the poor to offer their pigeons to God.

I did not expect that this vision would continue. I was surprised to see the vision again. The following week the vision of our church members appeared again on the wall at the same spot. Everything was dark and only the area of the vision was bright. This time I saw or perceived that we were lacking in prayers. Prayers to God were poor among us.

We were very close to each other and loved each other. There was love in our small church. But in the eyes of God our prayers were poor. Any group of people and any society of their own groups can be in love and unity. Without prayers church is not different from such groups. The church is connected to God through prayers. Our church had a good relationship among ourselves horizontally, but a poor relationship vertically with

God. Prayer is practical faith in the Lord. Our church at the half basement lacked prayers. So I prepared a message about prayers.

After the Sunday message about prayers I observed any improvement in prayers among us. The answer was no. I blamed myself for delivering an ineffective, poor message about prayers. So I prepared and delivered a Sunday message again about prayers. I noticed that everybody remained the same in their prayer life.

This time I did not blame myself. I learned that people's prayer life will not change by Sunday messages no matter how many times I preach about prayers. Only action was needed. If I want to teach a soldier how to fight with many words, the soldier still does not know how to fight. But when I put the soldier in real battle, he will learn how to fight quickly. One action is better than a hundred preacher's words. Just do it. Just pray.

So I set up prayer meetings and prayed together with our prayer topics. When a church member faces an impossible or near impossible situation, we all together raise our prayers to God and overcome the impossible situation. Once a person goes through the struggles of prayers, and receives God's answer, he or she becomes a soldier of prayer and knows how to fight and win victory with prayers.

In this way, I gained confidence in delivering Sunday messages and preparing Sunday messages was a great joy. But the vision stopped after the second vision. There was no more vision at night. I kept the room dark and waited, waited, and waited with my eyes closed to see the vision but to no avail. It seemed like God would not show the vision of our church any more. I realized that God wanted me to grow in spiritual ability to discern the weakness of our church and overcome it with the words of Sunday messages. I was really sorry about this God's decision. But the Lord was firm and I had to accept that I must grow myself in spiritual insight to discern the spiritual condition of our church.

What should I do in order to grow in spiritual discernment? Should I pray? I began to pray for each church member one by one. Both visions were about our relationship with God, and our attitude toward God. When can I see the spiritual condition of the church in one glance?

Through these experiences I understood what church is. Church is like a ship on its voyage. All kinds of different people are on the ship. Although they are all different, they share one thing together. The course of their voyage is the same. Sunday's message is the navigator of the ship. The destination of the ship is heaven through Jesus.

Some ships follow the right courses toward heaven growing in the right relationship with God, growing in the image of Jesus and all arrive safely to heaven's gate. Some ships are lost, wandering around and all people in the ship wander around together. Some ships are in a shipwreck and all people in the ship face the shipwreck. A pastor of a ship has to be vigilant to know which way the ship is going and navigate it to the right direction through Sunday messages.

After this, I faced another problem in preparing Sunday messages. For example, suppose that I saw the need of our church not one but two problems at the same time. Suppose that our church needs faith and love. Then I couldn't decide which one I should choose for that Sunday. Should I preach about faith? Should I preach about love? I wasted time because I could not choose one. I did not want to make a mistake but to choose the right one.

Then I had a dream. In my dream I had two kinds of meat, beef and chicken, on a cutting board in the church kitchen to cook for church members. I had a knife in my hand. But I did not know which meat I was going to cook. I was wondering about between beef or chicken, beef or chicken, not being able to choose one. As I was wasting time between beef or chicken, the church members arrived to eat, and I did not even cut the meat.

Thank goodness. I woke up and it was a dream. I was relieved from the desperate situation. But I found a solution to my problem. I should choose one meat and cook it this week. Next week I can cook the other one. How easy it is! So I overcame the problem.

After this I had no more education about Sunday messages from God. But I constantly put my effort into improving my Sunday messages. It generally goes through four stages.

1. Choosing a suitable passage for the need of church I learned this through two visions.

2. First, receiving the words in my own heart I tried to listen to the words of God directly from the Bible. That was the best way but it did not always happen. Then I read Calvin's commentaries. It is written in old English but I was inspired by reading them. God has to open my heart and give me the meaning of the words I meditate. In this period, I

experienced death and resurrection; death because I did not understand the words of God, resurrection when God gives me the meaning of the words into my heart. So God's message moves from heart to heart, from my heart to the audiences' hearts.

3. Writing after I understand the meaning of the words of God and my heart is filled with spirit and power, I have to write it in human words. I pray several times to get help from the Lord. I pray for 'what to write and how to write.' I pray to write it in simple, clear, and powerful ways so that the meaning of God's words may not be complicated. I also look at the meaning of God's words from the audience's perspective. Viewing an object from above is different from viewing it from below. When this part is well done, the audience will think: "That's me. The words of God is talking about me." Then he applies the words of God to his real life. I approach only 80-90% of the audience's perspective and leave the rest 20-10% to be realized on their own.

4. Delivery of the message in the presence of the Holy Spirit A messenger has to capture the audience' attention within a few minutes at the beginning and guides them into the words of God for the next 30 minutes toward a conclusion of one word or one core teaching. At the end of the message one word or one point remains in the heart of the audience. That's their spiritual food for one week.

This is my way of preparing the Sunday message.

Why did God come to the empty half basement? There was nothing nice looking inside. My half basement was the poorest of all the poor half basements. Did the Lord come because it was the poorest?

In my opinion, the reason that the Lord came was that we were doing what the Lord asked us to do; preach the words! Had I spent my money, time, and my mind to decorate the place, would the Lord have visited? Had I spent my time and mind to entertain my feelings and emotions, would the Lord have come?

The Lord came because He was pleased with us. He came because we were doing what the Lord asked us to do; preach the words! (2 Timothy 4:2) God saves people through the words and believers must preach the words so that God may work through the words. So every believer should teach the words of God to family members, to friends, neighbors, and even to strangers. But it seems like it is normal not to teach the Bible because it is considered to be the job of pastors. I went to a Christians' meeting. With all their sincerity and devotion of their hearts they were doing everything except teaching the Bible. I was questioning in my heart; what are you doing? You are doing everything except what the Lord asked you to do.

What does it mean that God came to the half basement? When a president of a nation visits a struggling local region, does he just come to stop by? No. He brings a package with him to develop the area. God did not just stop by. God had a package for the half basement.

Chapter 5:
Two of You

A woman missionary, Young, arrived from Korea. My courage was doubled by her presence. Soon she got a job as a nursing aide at a nursing home near the airport. She was a R.N. in Korea. She had to work as a nursing aide with a temporary work permit until she could pass the nurse board examination for R.N. of the State of Ohio. We had a little dispute about our rent. I said that I had to pay more because I make more money as a R.N. and she makes less money as an aide. She insisted that we have to split the rent equally because she uses half of the apartment. I lost in this argument and we split the rent equally. Otherwise, we worked together as one heart to serve the Lord.

She did not have a car and she did not know how to drive. Both of us worked the evening shift so that both of us could go to work with one car. When we went to work, we left home early. I drove near to the airport and dropped her off at the nursing home. Then I drove back to the city to my work which was near downtown. At the end of the work at around 11 pm, I drove back to the nursing home near the airport to pick her up. When we arrived home in the half basement after midnight, we ate and started to pray together. One person was praying and the other person almost fell asleep. When that person finished her prayer, the other person started to pray. After this prayer we went to bed. We prayed mainly to give us college students' ministry.

Three months passed. I was driving almost 100 miles a day when both of us went to work. And Young was not thinking about being independent by taking driving lessons and buying her own car. It seemed that getting a ride to her work was granted. I did not ask her for a gas fee. I was physically exhausted. My face and eyes were swollen because of tiredness. I still had to teach the words of God, and prepare Sunday messages. Did she come to help me or to be a burden on me? I did not know how long she was going to depend on my driving for her work. I just could not go on like this anymore. I gave her an ultimatum; "I will give you three months to have a driver's license, buy your own car and be independent for your work. If not, move out of here."

I did not know how to say it diplomatically. I put everything in the hand of the Lord.

The next morning we avoided seeing each other directly. But we had to talk and see each other. She said that she came to America as a missionary and she would stay to serve God. She would get driver's license and her own car in three months. It seemed like she cried all night silently. Her two eyes and eyelids were red and swollen like pine cones. She was from a rich family and such harsh words from me might have been hard on her. I knew that she died in her pride and rose as a new person to live her life to serve God. Thank the Lord for His grace upon us. I could not bear her burden any more. She wept probably all night. But the Lord brought two of us together.

She began to have driving lessons. And in less than three months she drove her own car!!!! All together I drove almost 6 months for her work. After this she was a different person. She devoted herself to serve God as a missionary with me. She and I had one week off from work and had a Genesis conference Monday through Friday in our half basement. I delivered a message each day in English and Young drew a picture according to the content of the message and posted it on the wall. I invited students and people in the apartment building and every day someone came and listened to my message. She wanted me to do my best in serving the Lord and I felt pressure from her to serve the Lord better. She also did her best to serve the Lord.

"Again, I tell you that if two of you on earth agree about anything you ask for, it will be done for you by my Father in heaven. For where two or three come together in my name, there am I with them." **Matthew 18:19,20**

Here, Jesus mentioned 'two of you' and 'two or three.' In written words it is simple. In reality it takes months or years to reach 'two of you agree' and 'two or three come together.' It does not mean two people come together physically. It means that two different hearts are united into one heart to serve the Lord.

I used to walk one hour to go to work. I walked back another hour after work. No one gave me a ride to work. But I did not ask her to walk as I did. I had to die to serve her by driving for her so that she could work. She had to die in her pride and dignity to meet my demand. The reason I drove for six months was to serve God. The reason she decided not to leave but to get a car was to serve God. So two of us agreed, two of us came together in Jesus' name. It took us six months to be two of us. Ever since I felt that she and I had one heart. Without speaking I could read her mind and she could read my mind. Two of us prepared Bible studies, Sunday worship services, and prayed together.

But not many were as lucky as Young and me. Many faced irreconcilable situations and separated. Going solo was a better choice. There would be no more dispute, no more conflict, and no disagreement. That was what I saw that many missionaries preferred to work as a solo. And they were working very hard, sacrificing many personal lives to serve the Lord.

I want to write Matthew 18:19, 20 as a mathematical formula.

Working as a solo $1+0 = 1$ (working very hard, sacrificing many personal lives, tired)

Working as two $1+1 =$ It will be done for you by my Father in heaven.

There am I with you.

$1+1$ is not 2. $1+1=$ God's power, Jesus' presence

I don't know why God works with 'two of you' or 'two or three of you' but God works that way.

"Calling the Twelve to him, he sent them out two by two and gave them authority over evil spirits." **Mark 6:7**

"After this the Lord appointed 72 others and sent them two by two ahead of him to every town and place where he was about to go." **Luke 10:1**

The disciples imitated whatever Jesus did. I am sure that they learned to work two by two and not as a solo. Peter and John competed to be the first. But after Jesus' death and resurrection, before the task of preaching the Gospel to the end of the earth, there was no room in their hearts for men's pride, ambition, competition, and leadership position. Peter and John joined in their hearts as 'two of you' to carry on the task of world evangelization.

As I was preparing my retirement from the church I focused on one thing; making 'two of you' 'two or three come together.' Church built on 'two of you' has the power of God. Church on 'two or three come together' has the presence of Jesus with them. It was done over ten years slowly and surely. And it was done. Our leadership brothers have one heart to serve God. They know each other's heart without words. They encourage each other to serve the Lord better. I retired in peace.

Chapter 6:
Jimmy

One young college student came to the half basement to study the Bible. His name was Jimmy (not real name). He came from Lebanon. When the Lebanese Civil War broke out, his parents sent him to America with $5000. He was admitted at the University of Toledo as a student and he rented his apartment in the same apartment building where I lived. I invited him to Bible study and he came.

When he came into our half basement, he stayed less than two or three feet from the door. He never advanced further than that. In the apartment where two Korean women were living, he stayed at the door. We put a small table and a chair near the door. We called it 'Jimmy's chair. I taught him Genesis. When he studied the Bible, he said that his girlfriend would be angry at him if she knew he was studying the Bible. So I thought that his girlfriend was a Moslem. Jimmy came and sat in his chair even when there was no Bible study. We did not lock the apartment door so he could come in any time he wanted.

One day he showed me his mouth. He had red sores in both corners of his mouth. He was worried about it. I immediately knew that he had vitamin C deficiency. I bought a bag of apples and gave it to him. Several days later he came smiling happily. He showed me that the sores were healing,

One day he told me about his problem. He was running out of money. He almost used $5000 his parents gave him. After he paid the first semester tuition and paid the apartment, he did not have enough money to cover the next semester. He could not continue studying and maintain his student's visa in America.

He had a friend in Canada and he decided to go to Canada. He said that he could work as a gas station attendant in Canada. In order to go to Canada he had to receive some paper from the Lebanese consulate in Detroit. He asked me to help him with two things; to drive to the Lebanese consulate in Detroit, and to pretend as if I were his girlfriend at the consulate. He explained the reason. Lebanese men are rude and harsh to another Lebanese man. But in front of women, they act nicely to give a good impression. Without me they may reject his paper. With me they may give the paper. I agreed to help him with these.

On the day of his appointment at the consulate, I put on the best clothes I had. I drove with Jimmy to the Lebanese consulate in Detroit. We entered the office of the consulate. I sat on a chair in the office while Jimmy was processing his papers. There were about 3 men working at the office. Things went smoothly and they gave Jimmy the paper for him to go to Canada. We returned to Toledo. Jimmy went to his apartment and I returned to my half basement. That was the last time I saw Jimmy. I thought that he might have entered Canada safely. Otherwise, he would have come to my half basement and sat in his chair at the door.

When Jimmy was with us, we never talked about the civil war, why they were killing each other, who were fighting against whom. We never talked about religion, about Christianity and Moslem. Our hearts were on Jimmy and worried about him. He should be studying in college in Lebanon and live with his family. But the civil war changed the fate of their precious son overnight. He became an international orphan like a fallen leaf drifting away swept by a strong current of a war.

God gave us a special meaning about Jimmy. Young had a dream. In her dream our half basement apartment door was flung open widely. Jimmy walked in with a big smile on his face and followed after Jimmy, American students were coming into our half basement and she did not see the end. Jimmy was the herald of the coming college students' ministry. We were praying for college students' ministry and it started with Jimmy. Jimmy was our first college Bible student. Through this dream, Young and I knew that God had a plan to start college students' ministry in the half basement. In reality it happened after one and a half years through my future husband.

Why are there war after war? The ultimate solution to human problems is fighting and killing. Obviously one side is wrong and the other side is violated. But it does not matter who is right and wrong. Justice should be the solution, but it is not. The solution is fighting until one kills the other. The winner is the one who has weapons that can kill more people. Winner is the killer.

When I was young, my parents taught me to do the right things. I would be a winner by doing the right thing. I would be a loser when I do the wrong thing. But as I grew, I saw more and more that I live in a world where a killer is the winner. But I still keep my parent's teaching and value of being a winner by doing the right things. Even by doing so I cannot stop wars, But God can stop wars, only God can do it.

God speaks about an unbelievable future for humans. There will be peace in the world.

"In the last days

The mountain of the Lord's temple will be established as chief among the mountains;

It will be raised above the hills, and all the nations will stream to it.

Many peoples will come and say,

"Come, let us go up to the mountain of the Lord, to the house of the God of Jacob.

He will teach us his ways, so that we may walk in his paths."

The law will go out from Zion, the word of the Lord from Jerusalem.

He will judge between the nations and will settle disputes for many peoples.

They will beat their swords into plowshares and their spears into pruning hooks.

Nation will not take up sword against nation, nor will they train for war anymore. **Isaiah 2:2-4**

Nations will learn from God and God's ways.

God will judge between nations and settle disputes. That means that international problems will be solved by justice, not by killings. Since problems will be solved according to justice, there will be no need for weapons, no need for drafting and training men as soldiers.

Until then wars will continue. Wars will change the fate of precious sons and daughters overnight. Jimmy, I miss you. Good luck, Jimmy.

Chapter 7:

It Is Eleven O'clock

It was a winter blizzard. The cold temperature was more of a problem than snow. I worried about going to work for both Young and I. I got up in the morning and went out to the parking lot.

I tried to start the engine of my car but the engine did not start. I returned to my half basement. I called AAA for help because I was a member of AAA. They were getting so many phone calls for help and there was a long waiting list. They might be able to come to help me after three days. The only source to get help for my car was not available.

I was thinking about what to do. 'I will do my best to start the car and go to work. If the car does not start, both Young and I have to notify work in time so that our workplaces can adjust scheduling.' I hate to miss my work. Work schedule is a contract between my employer and me. They expect me to work and I have responsibility to work as scheduled. As long as I was alive, I went to work. Both Young and I worked the evening shift.

At least by 11 AM I should know whether I could go to work or not. Legally I had to notify the nursing office two hours before work starts if I had to miss work but I wanted to know earlier than two hours.

That day I invented the most powerful spiritual weapon of hourly prayer. I decided to pray every hour. There are prayer meetings once a month, once a week, and daily. But I had not yet seen hourly prayer. So I decided to pray every hour at 7AM, 8AM, 9AM, 10 AM, and 11AM. Hourly prayer was the most powerful spiritual weapon I experienced so far, and hourly prayer of two people is a 100% spiritual atomic bomb. There is no need for fasting. Just pray every hour 5-10 minutes till time to go to bed. It requires commitment and dedication that day.

"Again I tell you that if two of you on earth agree about anything you ask for, it will be done for you by my Father in heaven. For where two or three come together in my name, there am I with them." Matthew 18:19,20

After prayer I went out to the parking lot and tried to start the car. The car did not start. I opened the front hood of the car and saw the shiny frozen cold metal parts. I was thinking that God has power to start the car. When the power of God touches the metal parts, all the metals would move and work. I kept the hood open thinking the sunlight might warm up the engine and help the engine to start. Then I returned to my half basement.

After another hour I prayed that the car might start and went to the parking lot. It did not start. I repeated this every hour.

For the last 11AM prayer I started early. At 10:45AM I prayed. This would be the last prayer to start the car. If the car did not start this time, it wouldn't start. Both Young and I would have to call work. After the prayer I went to the parking lot and tried to start the car. It did not start. Well, my prayer was not answered. From the car I walked toward the entrance of the apartment building.

A man was walking several yards in front of me. He was walking in the same direction toward the entrance of the apartment building. He was wearing a camouflage army jacket with a hood over his head. I had not seen any soldiers living in the same apartment. I was curious to know who it was. I ran, passed him, and turned back to see his face.

He was an old white man. He said to me; "Do you have trouble starting your car?" I answered, "Yes." He said, "Let me help you." I was surprised by his words. "How in the world did he know my problem?" From that spot he turned back to the parking lot and I followed behind him. He already knew where my car was. He went to his car, drove his car, and parked his car next to mine. He connected his jumper cables from the battery of his car to the battery of my car. He asked me to go inside of my car and try to start the engine. I tried and it did not start. He said, "Try again." I repeated it a few more times, and finally it started with thick black smoke. He said that I flooded the engine with gas, causing thick black smoke to come out of the engine.

Still sitting in the driver's seat, I shouted loudly to him.

"Look at your watch! It is eleven o'clock!"

He heard my shouting and brought his arm to the window and showed me his wrist watch. I saw that the time was 11 o'clock 20 seconds. The engine started precisely at eleven o'clock. Didn't I ask the Lord to start the car at eleven? And that's what the Lord did exactly as I had asked. I explained to him how I prayed every hour to start the car at eleven o'clock.

As I was praying hourly, the Lord had already sent this man to the parking lot. The Lord guided him to see me standing beside my car with the front hood open. He might even have seen me trying to start the car but couldn't. Still he did not have an intention to help me, until I ran and looked at his face as if I was about to ask for help from him.

Until then I was thinking that the Lord helps me with His almighty power directly. Through this I learned another God's way of helping me besides direct almighty power. The Lord helps me by sending a suitable person, even a total stranger, who can help me. And I learned of course the power of hourly prayer.

Chapter 8:
Obscene Calls

Young and I were in the half basement apartment. Our landline phone rang. Young answered the phone. I heard what Young was talking on the phone. "What is that?" "Something sweet?"

"Oh! That's chocolate. You want chocolate." Then Young passed me the phone saying that someone wanted chocolates.

I got the phone and asked, "May I help you?" Over on the other side an American man said that he wants xxxxxx, one word that I had never heard of before. I apologized to him that I did not understand the word and asked him to repeat it to me. I still did not know the word and I asked Young to bring me an English-Korean dictionary. I asked the man over the phone. "Don't go. I will look for the word in the dictionary. Don't hang up, please." Young brought me an English Korean dictionary. I asked the American man to tell me the spelling of the word. We wanted to find out what it was to help the American man. He started to tell us spellings of the word one by one. He started with 'F' and we opened the F section in the dictionary. I asked "Next?" He said, "L," we flipped the pages of the dictionary. The word he spelled was floozy. I quickly read the Korean translation. It was a loose woman, a street woman. I hung up the phone right away.

I never knew the words obscene calls and never knew such a thing existed in the world. Phone calls I knew had to be sincere and honest conversation with respect to the other side.

After a few weeks later our phone rang. I picked up the phone, saying "Hello?" On the other side an American man was breathing rapidly and was not able to talk discernibly. Immediately I thought that he had a heart attack and needed help urgently. I asked him, "Do you need help?"

He managed to answer faintly, "Yes." I asked him, "How may I help you?" He said, "It is growing." In a split second I thought it was a little weird to describe the heart attack pain as growing. It should be 'it is getting worse' instead of 'it is growing.' But I quickly imagined that chest pain was growing into four chambers of his heart.

I turned to a rescue mode to save this dying man from a heart attack. He had difficulty breathing. I should not delay helping him. From the beginning he should have asked for an ambulance but he did not ask for it. I finally said what he should have said, "Do you want me to call an ambulance for you?" Suddenly he was fully recovered, breathing normally, and talking normally; "No-www. I need you." I hung up the phone.

I could guess who it was. It was a young man who lived in the same apartment building. I invited him to Bible study and I gave him my phone number. I could not tell who would respond to Bible study or who would respond with obscene calls. This was America. I had to deal with it.

I prepared some words to answer in case he calls again. The words I prepared were 'Go to a mental hospital. Go to a police station.'..... etc. There was no caller ID and I had to answer when the phone rang. He called again and again.

And there was another man that bothered me. One day I went to the college dormitory to meet my Bible student for Bible study. The male college student and I made an appointment to study the Bible at his dormitory room. At the appointed time I entered the dormitory building. His room was on the second floor. When I was still on the first floor, he called me from the second floor. I looked up. Lo and behold! He stood there, his upper body naked but lower part wrapped with white towel. It seemed like he just came out of the shower.

I smelled flesh in my spirit. He was not a man on his way for Bible study, but like a man on his way to a bodybuilders' competition. I don't care about men's muscles. What I look at in man is the quality of his brain and what's on his mind. Anyway I waited until he put on his clothes. We studied the Bible in his dormitory room with the door open, but the Bible study did not go well. Since then I distanced him but he continued to come to our church.

For this reason, I do not recommend a single unmarried young woman going abroad as a missionary. Before seeing a dream of mission come true she could meet a tragedy. When I went to Korea to get married, and got married, I told my husband about these two men. And my husband took care of them. They never showed up again. I finally felt safe. When I became a pastor later, I made it a policy not to teach the Bible or care for the opposite sex. Men take care of other men, and women take care of other women.

Chapter 9:
Marriage

As I was very busy with work, Bible studies, and Sunday worship services, the church leader called me from Korea to come to Korea to get married. He asked, "Do you want to see his picture?" I said, "No. I don't need to see his picture. You don't have to send me his picture." The reason why I refused the picture of my future husband was my faith in the Lord. I believed that God has chosen the suitable person for me. God brought Eve to Adam. (Genesis 2:22) God brought Rebekah to Issac. (Genesis 24:15) God will lead me to a man God chose for me. Besides, my two personal preferences for a future husband were satisfied. He was a servant of God, and he was smart. He majored in physics at Seoul National University. So why do I need to see his picture?

I had a vacation about less than two weeks from work. I could not be away for many days because of Bible studies and Sunday worship services. I had no substitute person to replace me during my trip. I left on Monday so that I might miss just one Sunday worship service. There was no direct flight from Toledo to Korea. I had to go from Toledo to Chicago by Greyhound bus. From Chicago O'Hare airport I flew to Korea. I bought round trip flight tickets between O'Hare airport and

Gimpo airport and round trip bus tickets between Chicago to Toledo.

I did not have any decent clothes to wear. I did not buy any new clothes in America except nursing uniforms. I bought a few clothes from thrift stores and wore them repeatedly. For the trip I bought a white T-shirt with red stripes for $3. I wore white nursing uniform pants with a T-shirt and wore white nursing shoes. After these preparations I had $5 left in my hand.

I did not want to borrow money. When I don't have money now and borrow money, how am I going to pay it later? Also, I had no one from whom I could ask to lend me money. 'If you don't have money, don't do it.' That was my rule. But I did not apply that rule to my marriage. No rule prevented an old maid from getting married.

I arrived in Chicago by Greyhound bus. There were a few hours before going to the airport. I stayed briefly at one apartment where few women missionaries stayed. They were mad at me.

"You look like a bagger. People in Korea will say that a beggar came from America. Not only you but also we would be considered as beggars as well because of you." I thought 'Do I look that bad?' Well, when you go to Korea, why don't you go in style?'

Anyway they gave me a ride to the airport for my flight. After a long flight I arrived at the airport in Korea. After I went through customs, I walked through the exit to the lobby. Church brothers and sisters were waiting and welcomed me. Among them one brother was holding a flower bundle in his hand. So I knew he was the one I would get married to. He was very, very handsome. The flowers were yellow marigolds which can be found easily in homes and sidewalks. Every single flower withered, dropped its head and the wrapping paper was thick white paper which is used for copy machines.

I immediately figured out what he had done with the flowers. He wanted to give me flowers but did not have money. He picked the flowers from a garden or a sidewalk. He should have kept them in water for a while but he didn't. By the time I arrived, all the flowers withered. And the wrapping paper! He must have taken it out from the church copy machine. Anyway I appreciated and enjoyed his effort and unpolished presentation of the flower bundle for me. I myself arrived with $5 cash and wore nursing uniform pants and shoes.

Since I had no money I could not travel to my home in Mokpo. My family in Mokpo did not have a phone. I called a pharmacy in my neighborhood in Mokpo and asked them to bring my parents to their phone which they did. I just told my parents and I came to Seoul to get married. After that I had nothing to do since I did not have money. But I did not worry.

I prepared my marriage with the words of God. I studied the words of Genesis 2:18-25 about marriage in the Garden of Eden. I taught these words many times for others but this time I studied for my own marriage. The Garden of Eden means paradise, the ultimate happiness for humans. And the center of the paradise was marriage. How precious it is! I am about to receive this happiness in my own life.

"So the Lord God caused the man to fall into a deep sleep, and while he was sleeping, he took one of the man's ribs and closed up the place with flesh. Then the Lord God made a woman from the rib he had taken out of the man, and he brought her to the man.

The man said,

"This is now bone of my bones and flesh of my flesh; She shall be called 'woman' for she was taken out of man."

Genesis 2:21-23

This was the happiest marriage, the first marriage in the Garden of Eden. God made the woman out of the man and brought her to the man. The man received her as a part of himself.

The marriage of Adam and Eve was so beautiful that I felt happy. I was about to meet a man from whom I was made.

Late in the evening my man came to visit me. I could not see him straight. So I looked at the floor of the room. He talked about himself, his faith in the Lord, and his family. I just listened and I could not say a word. Since then he came every evening. On the third evening we went out to have tea together.

This marriage in the Garden of Eden has been changed, evolved, commercialized, and inflated. Humans made marriage very complicated and difficult. There are so many requirements and poor people cannot get married. It costs them so much money: bridal preparation, wedding dress, invitation cards, photo sessions, wedding ceremony, rings, reception place, foods & drinks, flowers, limousine, new furniture, new place to live, honeymoon...

Also humans removed God's truth from marriage. Without God's truth marriage crumbles down no matter how much money they pour for their marriage.

In this passage there are all the principles and secrets for a happy marriage. Even though the paradise was lost, husband and wife still can have a happy married life when they return to the truth of marriage and apply the principles written in this chapter. Every man and woman should study this passage before their marriage to understand why and how God established marriage in the Garden of Eden.

I received the words of Genesis 2:25, "The man and his wife were both naked, and they felt no shame." This means being naked literally. But also it means that there is no secret between them. Secrets in marriage life build an invisible wall between husband and wife. They cannot become one flesh. (Genesis 2:24) And the marriage will eventually be torn apart. I decided that I would keep no secret between my husband and me. There will be no secret in my marriage life.

My family arrived from Mokpo to Seoul. My sister opened her 7 years savings and used it for my marriage expenses. I had two days to prepare for the wedding with the money my sister brought.

I went to a market called East Gate. I bought a one piece dress, shoes, and a hat because the sun was very hot. My outlook totally changed when I put them on. My man liked my new look. He said that I looked like Julie Andrews in the movie 'The Sound of Music.' Julie Andrews was a tall white

American actress and I was a short Asian woman. He meant that my personality was like Maria, whom Julie Andrews played in the movie. I bought gifts for his family and a watch as a wedding gift for my husband. I rented a wedding dress. I don't remember the wedding date but it was the third week Thursday of August in 1976.

We married in our church before brothers and sisters with singing hymns, prayers, and blessings. Brothers and sisters decorated inside of the church for our wedding. I was grateful for their love and efforts.

Church leaders gave me about 6-7 books as a wedding gift. In all my life, I did not see people give books as wedding gifts. Don't people give money as wedding gifts? I don't give books as wedding gifts to others. Did they receive books for their own weddings? Do their sons and daughters receive books as wedding gifts? Seeing that all the gifts were books, a direction must have been given and everyone followed it. All book wedding gifts conveyed a message to me. The message was felt in my heart. The message I felt was 'You don't deserve more than this.' The reason might be that I left NY on my own.

My travel bag did not have wheels at the bottom. I carried my heavy bag on my shoulder with the books. I carried the books from Korea all the way to Toledo. I did not open it and did not see who gave me the books. I put them somewhere in my half basement and they were gone.

We went on our honeymoon to a mountain resort. When we arrived at the hotel room, I asked my husband to take out all the money he had and put them on the bed. I also put out all the money I had on the bed. I put them together and counted to know how much money we had all together. I calculated our expenses for the honeymoon for two nights and three days. I put aside my expenses for my return trip to America, little money to buy gifts on our return. With the rest of the money we could eat one regular meal with rice but the rest we had to eat cheap noodles and ramen. I never heard a story of starving couples during their honeymoon, but we could have been the first case of starving honeymooners unless I had budgeted the cost of meals.

The next day my husband and I left the hotel to spend the day. On the road side an old man was renting old bicycles. My husband rented one bicycle for one hour and I sat on the seat behind holding his back. He was riding on the unpaved road and I worried whether we might have a flat tire because of our weight. I was relieved when we returned the bicycle without any damage. There were commercial photographers on the road for the newlyweds but we did not take any pictures because we did not have extra money. So we don't have honeymoon pictures.

He started to walk toward the top of the mountain and I followed behind him. We walked along the uphill road with rocks and dirt. It was so hot without any shade. I was sweating. Every activity cost money but walking on the mountain did not cost any money. At some point, we started to come down. When we came down the mountain, we went to a restaurant for dinner, a rice dinner! Side dishes were all vegetables and mushrooms from the mountain and tasted so good and fresh.

That day I was able to say to him what I wanted to say. He was an inspired poet. He has won several awards in poetry competitions since his high school. I was the opposite. I did not like poems and poets. I worried that in the future he might want me to read his poems and understand his world. Should I pretend to like his poems? Or should I tell him from the start that I did not like poems and poets? I was debating this in my mind. I decided to make it very clear from the start. I said to him; "I don't like poems and poets. Please, keep your poems for yourself and don't ask me to read them." He just listened to what I said.

When we returned from the honeymoon, we had to register our marriage at the American embassy before my departure. But we found that my uncle in Busan sent us a wrong family certificate. They did not send the family registry certificate in my name but in my sister's name.

So my husband hurried to go to Busan by train and returned with the right certificate the next day. One day before my departure we were able to report our marriage at the American embassy at Seoul. There was a registration fee which I did not know about. I emptied my pocket and I had just the right amount of money to pay the registration fee and had 10 cents left. The ten cents was the expense I had to travel back from Korea to Toledo. Can I return home with ten cents? But why not? At least I secured a return flight ticket and a bus ticket.

I left Korea and arrived at O'Hare airport in Chicago. Again there were a few hours between the arrival of the flight and the departure of the Greyhound bus to Toledo. I stayed a couple of hours at one missionary's home who gave me a ride to the Greyhound bus station. It was late evening and the bus was running all night for about 7-8 hours stopping by several places. I was very, very hungry. The last time I ate and drank was inside of the airplane of the Korean Airline. I did not eat for more than half a day. I had no money to buy something to eat when the bus stopped. I could not buy anything with one dime.

In the bus behind me sat a group of Germans. They were eating cookies. I turned around and said to a German woman, "Ich bin hunger." She quickly gave me two cookies. The two cookies were life-saver for me. Even though my German was incorrect, she understood what I meant.

Anyway I left America with $5 to get married, I got married to a man whom God chose for me, and returned with 10 cents. The Lord provided my need and made everything possible.

I was not sure whether I should write about my marriage because it was not a pleasant story. But I decided to share it because I want to comfort those who did not have enough money for their marriage and honeymoon.

Chapter 10:
Ministry of American College Students

I returned to Toledo after my marriage in Korea. I had to catch up with Bible studies and Sunday worship service. Meanwhile four new women missionaries arrived from Korea. They were all married and waiting for their husbands to come to America. The half basement was crowded. They stayed in the half basement until they found their own apartments.

I continued what I had been doing, working a full time job, teaching the Bible, and preaching on Sundays. As the number of church members increased, I had to handle more small and big problems. I was stretched very thin and began to feel a lack of leadership and power. I wanted the church to grow. But when the church was growing, I was overwhelmed by so much work I had to do. I felt my limit. To most people, working one full time job is enough. I was working one full time job as a nurse and a full time pastor's job.

In the Garden of Eden, God made a man to do the work in the garden. Man has an ability to see the whole situation and power to know what to do. God created a woman as his helper. Women are delicate, sensitive, and detailed. She supports a man who works on a large scale. So men are macromanagers while women are micromanagers.

I realized this truth deeply in my heart. How true it is. I was created as a helper but was doing a man's job. This would be corrected when my husband comes and works as the main worker, and I work as his helper. I waited for my husband to come and take over the ministry. But it took a long time and he arrived almost after one year.

Not long after his arrival, my husband went to a Christian meeting and met a young American man whom my husband invited to our half basement. He came to our half basement and he liked our church. He began to invite his friends. Several of his friends came. They invited their friends, college students. My husband devoted himself to teaching the words of God to raise them as Bible teachers. I also taught the words of God to female college students. Other women missionaries also devoted themselves to teaching American college students. The demography of our church was changing from Koreans to American college students. Korean middle aged men and women left but young Koreans remained and adopted the college students' ministry.

Tables for Bible study increased from one to three so that three teams could study the Bible at the same time in the half basement. Still we did not have any furniture. Students rested sitting or lying on the carpet. Since there was only one space, whenever we ate, we could not eat just for ourselves. We invited students in the room to eat together with us. Almost every dinner we shared our food with someone. Most church doors were locked and opened just on weekends. But the students could come to our half basement 24/7 anytime.

One night my husband and I were sleeping. One student knocked on the door. I opened the door. He said that he had something to talk to my husband about. So we turned the light on and he came in to talk to my husband. I just turned myself toward the wall to avoid the light and go back to sleep. Ever since I went to bed in street clothes because students came in at any time at night. I did not want to show myself in pajamas.

One Sunday my husband was preaching during Sunday worship service. I was sitting on one of the chairs. I happened to turn my head to the left, and through the window on the ground level outside I saw a young man and a woman were holding each other and rolling over the lawn. I quickly turned my head toward my husband so as not to distract his preaching. Soon after I wanted to see outside again to see whether they were still there. When I looked outside, they were still rolling with two bodies and four legs tangled together… Not only I but others also might have seen the rolling couple. That day I did not remember the words of the Sunday sermon, but remembered the rolling couple deep in my heart like a short clip of a video.

I was thankful to our students who sought God's truth in such an environment. Selling and buying drugs was a common scene. Young girls were pregnant and had babies. In such a decadent environment our precious Bible students fixed their hearts on the words of God and prayers. They decided to live their lives dedicated to God. They came to the half basement to worship the Lord on Sunday, rejecting all kinds of fun activities.

My first daughter was born. One student liked to stay in the half basement and did not go home at night. Then we hung a sheet in the middle of the room. On one side of the sheet my husband, I, and my infant daughter slept on the carpet floor and on the other side the student slept on the carpet floor with a blanket. Then my husband said to me about the student, "His home is like a mansion but he wants to sleep here on the floor."

Our American students repented their sins and lived a new life as Bible teachers. They began to teach the words of God to other students. We stayed in the half basement for around 3 years. There were so many that we had to move out. My family rented a two bedroom duplex on the second floor. We had more rooms and more spaces. Our family could have one room for ourselves. But tenants who lived downstairs were annoyed by noises we made.

We were practicing Christmas hymns. Someone knocked on the door. It was a policeman. The tenants downstairs complained about the noises to the police. Police gave us a warning not to make noises anymore saying, "if I come back again, you will go downtown." Downtown meant a jail. I wished that we stopped practicing Christmas Hymns. But my husband continued. Strangely the police did not return even though we continued practicing Christmas hymns.

But another police came with another problem. Police received a report that someone was shouting for help from our apartment. One brother was praying. This was his prayer style; he shouted loudly HELP! Then prayed quietly…, loudly, HELP! Then quiet prayer…, loudly HELP! Then quiet prayer…, loudly HELP. So the tenant downstairs heard only occasional loud HELP! We explained to the police that a brother was praying and asking God for help.

Anyway our students' Bible teachers raised other students as Bible teachers. The number of students kept increasing and we had to move out to a bigger place. The church was growing but did not have enough money to have its own place. Our family and the church still had to be together.

The next time we rented a big single house. The house was located in an affluent neighborhood. Our family rented the big house and still the church was with us together. A dozen cars of our students parked in the street in front of the house. Their cars were old, rusted, almost junk, and they did not blend with the rich neighbors. It must have been an eyesore to the neighbors. Eventually we heard that the neighbors hired a lawyer to sue us. So we had to move out again to avoid legal problems. By this time, my husband was thinking about buying a place for the church.

He found a three story house near the campus. It had spacious land around the house. The church put a sum of money as a down payment. I don't remember the exact amount of money because I was not involved. Next two years monthly rent would be credited to the principal. After two years the church had to come up with the rest balance of the purchase price with either loan or cash. It was called a land contract. So this three story house was bought and we moved out of the rich neighbors before tangling in a legal problem. The house was bought by the church. Our family paid the rent to the church. Finally peace came to our church. We had our own place and no other houses around us. We could sing and shout.

We stayed there until we found a problem. The three story house was about 3 or 5 degrees tilted. In order to try to save money my husband did not hire a home inspector before the purchase. A home inspector might have found that problem. The church had to give up the down payment and had to move out again. We lived there for more than two years. So I think that the land contract was nullified and the church lost the down payment. I think the church stayed just as tenants. Because of this Korean missionaries did not trust my husband who caused financial loss of church money.

Around that time, our family finally separated from the church and moved to a rental home.

After one year of renting a house we finally bought our own home. Looking back I moved seven times until we bought our home.

My husband found an empty storage building with a parking lot. The building was big, maybe 150 - 200 people could meet. The building was dilapidated and uninhabitable. When it rained, rain water dropped here and there from the roof inside of the building. But my husband saw its potential if repaired. It was close to the University of Toledo. It had a parking space. It was cheap. $30,000. It required a 10% down payment to buy which was $3,000. Some Korean missionaries refused to donate their money for the down payment mentioning the loss of money from the previous three story house. So out of desperation we put our only family car for sale. I posted at the hospital newspaper at my work and one of my coworkers bought it right away. With the money my husband bought the building and the parking lot.

Our American students were excellent handymen and experts on repairs. Several brothers went up to the roof, removed the old roof and replaced it with a new roof. Finally the church settled in its own place. Beginning from a half basement to this building it took 14 ½ years.

Other missionaries wanted to know the secret of building American college students' ministry.

How did he start? What did he do? What's the secret?

The answer was in 2 Samuel 7:1-16. When King David settled in a cedar palace, he felt sorry that the Lord stayed in a tent while he stayed in a cedar palace. He expressed his desire to build a house for the Lord. That night the Lord revealed what was in His heart. The heart of the Lord was touched by the desire of King David. God stayed in the tent and never asked the Israelites to build a house for the Lord. The Israelites did not think about God who stayed in a tent while they lived in palaces and mansions. David was the only one who was concerned about God's tent life. God was deeply moved by David's love for God.

God accepted David's desire to build the house of the Lord, but God did not want David to build the house of God. David was not suitable to build the house of God because he shed much blood as a warrior. (1 Chronicles 28:3) God chose Solomon to build the house of God and Solomon was not even born yet. (2 Samuel 7:13) I don't know when God decided to build the house of God, 20-30 years later Solomon began to build the temple.

So Solomon built the temple.

How did he start? What did he do? What is the secret?

But building the house of God was already decided by God before Solomon was born. (2 Samuel 7:12) Building the house of God was decided between God and David. It was decided because God's heart was touched by David's love for God.

What I am trying to say is that God already decided to allow American college students' ministry even before my husband arrived in Toledo, even before I married him. God revealed His decision through Young's dream. Young and I knew that college students' ministry was on the way. But not by us but someone else, who is suitable. I was a nurse and Young was a nurse aide. We were not suitable for young college students.

What moved the heart of the Lord to grant us college students' ministry? Was it because I drove with my left foot to go to Bible study after discharge from the hospital? Was it because I was teaching the Bible forgetting breakfast, lunch, and dinner? Was it because Young and I prayed every night till 1 AM for the campus ministry? I don't know. When I go to heaven, I have to ask the Lord. Anyway, more than two years of daily prayers had been accumulated before my husband came.

Starting a ministry starts in the heart of God. When God's heart is touched by our love, by our faith, by our prayers, by our sacrifices, God decides to grant it through a suitable person and at the right time. It is not by what we did with human method.

My husband had trouble with the church leader. The church leader invited him to the headquarters in Chicago. While my husband was in Chicago, a missionary in Toledo announced that he was the new director of the Toledo church. The next day the new director came to my house and said to us not to come to the Sunday worship service anymore. My husband did not know he was removed and the ministry was given to another man.

Chapter 11:

The Awesome Ocean

My home town Mokpo, a port city, is located at the south-west lower corner of the Korean peninsula. There are many small islands in the south western sea and many ships have arrived from these islands to Mokpo. Every summer there was news about casualties in the ocean such as drowning, capsizing of ships. Most of the victims were women and children who did not know how to swim.

My father felt that he should teach me how to swim. I was barely 5 or 6 years old. My father and I walked from home to the beach. We had to cross the Yudal mountain to reach the beach. He put me on top of a high cliff and I sat there. And my father went down to the sea and was swimming in the deep water near the cliff. That was my father's swimming lesson. He wanted me to watch him swim and learn how to swim. It was scary to look down into the deep ocean water from a high cliff but I was more worried about my father's safety than learning how to swim.

A few weeks later my father took me to the beach again to a shallow water where some little kids were playing in shallow water safely. I had a good time in the shallow ocean water jumping, running, riding the waves.

When my father took me to the beach again, I took a small rectangular plastic tube, the size of a pillow which I found at home. I inflated it by blowing the air into it with my mouth, held it with my two hands and I could float. The rectangular plastic tube was not meant for swimming but it supported my weight in the water. I had another level of fun with this tube. Moving my two legs constantly I moved around a wider area of the ocean but tried to stay in shallow water because I did not know how to swim.

Sometimes I checked the depth of the area I was playing. Holding the tube with my two hands I lowered my two feet into the ocean water to see whether I could touch the ocean bed with my feet. When I could not touch the bottom of the water with my two feet, I returned to the shallow water for safety. A few years passed and I still did not know how to swim but just had fun on the beach.

When I was having fun in the water I wanted to see the bottom of the sea with my eyes. I wanted to go down into the water but my body did not go down into the water. My body was just floating in the water. 'I want to see the bottom of the sea. But how am I going down to the bottom? My body keeps on floating and does not go down.' After many failures I realized that I have to dive with my head first. That was what other kids were doing. So I did the same like the other kids were doing. I took a deep breath, pushed my body straight up from the water and put my two hands and head down into the water. Finally I succeeded in going down into the ocean water to see the bottom of the sea with bare eyes. I saw not only the bottom of the sea but also many of the legs and feet of the kids.

Another time on the beach I was playing with the tube in the water. I lowered my feet into the water to measure the depth of the water where I was playing and my feet did not touch the ocean bottom. I was in a deep area. Suddenly I was scared. Then my body went down into the sea water vertically like a rock goes down into water. I held my little tube with two hands and quicked my two legs as fast as I could toward the shallow water.

I returned to the beach safely but I returned with a huge question. When I had fun in the water, my body kept on floating, I could not go down into the water and I had to dive in. When I had fear, my body sank down into the water vertically like a rock goes down. Why is that so? The salinity of the sea water is the same. My body mass is the same. My body weight is the same.

The only difference was fun or fear. When I had fun, my body did not go down. When I had fear, my body sank down. Why is that so?

What does fear play in this? Did fear paralyze not only my mind but also my body? Did fear make my body heavier?. In order to get an answer I experimented myself again later. I was convinced that fear indeed makes my body drown into the water. But why does fear make my body go down into the water? This question remained in my mind as homework. I did not find an answer to that question and I left my hometown and the ocean. This question remains unsolved all my life until today.

Still I learned a very valuable lesson for life in the ocean. 'When facing danger in the ocean, overcome fear first.' Fear may be a major cause of death in the ocean. People die when they don't have to die because of fear. When people are gripped with fear, they miss a chance of survival.

I finally learned how to swim. Several kids were playing in the shallow water randomly moving hands and feet in all directions. One coast guard or coast policeman came and watched us playing. He was the only one who wore goggles on the whole beach. He said that we were swimming in the wrong way. We asked him to teach us how to swim.

There was a swimming pool nearby and people could use it for a fee. He took us to that swimming pool for free and taught us how to move our arms and legs in coordination and how to lessen the water resistance. I followed his instructions several times and I got it. I finally began to swim. My goal was not only to swim fast but also to develop a beautiful swimming style. For so long I moved my hands and feet randomly with a lot of splashes. I came out of it. I paid attention to develop a beautiful swimming style. The attractive swimming style did not come from Olympic swimmers but came from Hollywood movies. The Hollywood movies showed the best swimming style to make the movie better. When I saw a very nice swimming style in a movie, I practiced repeatedly to make it my own.

The ocean is enormous and merciless. I was just one fish swimming in the ocean. People can lose their lives in split seconds in the ocean. In the ocean safety is number one.

The very basic safety in the ocean is knowing the tide. Is it high tide or low tide? During high tide the ocean water moves toward the beach and it carries swimmers to the beach. During low tide the ocean water moves away from the beach and it moves swimmers away from the beach. During low tide I swam in parallel with the coast line within safe distance. Actually I swam 10-15 degrees toward the beach in order to keep the parallel line with the beach. During high tide I swam directly toward the ocean. Still the waves carried me toward the beach and I could return to the beach very easily.

During low tide some swim directly toward the ocean. Nice! They may think that they swim very fast. No. It is the waves that carry them fast. They have to swim very very hard to return to the beach safely.

I began to go to the beach alone during weekends and summer vacations. At home I put on a swim suit and street clothes over it. I did not carry any water or snacks. I was going to swim just for swimming. My home was near the downtown area. I crossed the Yudal mountain and went to the beach. It was a long walk. On the beach I took off my t-shirt and skirt, put them in one place and jumped into the ocean water. I kept on swimming until I felt tired. When I was tired, I changed to backstroke position. Lying on my back on the water I rested while moving my hands and feet gently to stay afloat. I repeated swimming and resting in the ocean. Once I measured the time to see how long I was in the water. From the time I jumped into the water and to the time I came out, it was about two hours. Then I put on my clothes over my wet swimsuit and walked a long way back home.

One day while swimming I had a cramping in one of my legs. I could not swim because one leg was full of pain and stiffness. I was alone very far away from the beach. I had to overcome fear first. I said to myself. 'I will be okay. I will overcome this.' Confidence replaced fear in my heart in the middle of danger. I turned to the backstroke position. I managed to stay float by moving one hand. I lifted the cramping leg out of the water and massaged it with another hand. I had to massage even with two hands for a quick moment. After repeatedly massaging it my leg was eventually relieved from the cramping. I hated this cramping in the leg while swimming. But it happened again and I had to deal with it. It was life threatening because I could not swim in the middle of the ocean and it came without any warning.

In the beach there was a rope tied to buoys to mark the safe zone of swimming. The swimmers must stay within the rope. I was swimming near this rope and I did not go beyond the rope. Then suddenly I felt an excruciating pain in my stomach and I lost my balance. My body rolled over in the water, and almost fainted. I barely managed to approach the rope and held on to the rope. I had to overcome fear first. I said to myself, 'I will be okay. I will be able to overcome this.'

I held the rope with one hand and with another hand I began to massage my abdomen. The pain in my abdomen subsided gradually. I stayed there for a while hanging on the rope.

What had happened? What had caused so much pain? I did not know. My swimsuit was not torn. There were no bruises in my abdomen. Was it an electric shock by an electric eel? Was it a shock by a jellyfish? My best guess was maybe a big fish hit my abdomen with its sharp protruded mouth. I was swimming fast and a fish was coming fast hitting each other. Or the fish thought I was its food and tried to bite me. I could not imagine how I could have survived without the rope. The ocean is full of unexpected dangers.

Even though there were many unexpected dangers in the ocean, I still wanted to challenge the ocean more and more. I felt the whole ocean was for me and mine. I felt that I privately owned it and I was enjoying it to its full. People were swimming only in small areas. But I adventured to farther and newer areas.

That day I was swimming in a remote area of the beach. It was a part of the coast line but looked like an abandoned area covered with wild weeds. No one goes there. I swam there in parallel with the coast line to explore the area. While swimming I felt sharp pains in my legs. Every time I moved my legs I felt pain as if my legs were scratched by metal prongs. What's wrong? I realized that I was swimming on the seaweed patch. I saw that seaweeds were growing in the whole area but all the seaweeds remained about half feet under the water. Numerous small tiny sea shells covered the seaweed and my legs were scratched by the tiny sea shells.

The water where the seaweeds were growing was like swamp water and did not move. The principle of swimming did not work. The principle of swimming is that the body is going forward when water is pushed or squeezed backward and it does not work over the seaweed patch. After several strokes I should move several yards. But over the seaweed patch I was moving only a few feet instead of several yards. I realized that I was trapped over the seaweed patch and I was in real danger. There was no one around to ask for help.

I had to overcome fear first. I said to myself, 'I will be okay. I will overcome this.' My determination replaced fear in my heart. I needed to get out of there. Then which way should I swim to get out of the seaweed patch? I had to figure out the direction to get out. I noticed that the color of water over the seaweed patch was a little darker than the usual color of the ocean. That was the clue crucial to my safety. I had to find lighter colored ocean water and swim in that direction. I had to stand up to see the color of the water around me. So I pushed my body straight up. It was a very short time to look and I could see only one direction before my body came down into the seaweed patch. When my body went down into the seaweed patch, the tiny seashells scratched all over my legs. It was a pure torture. I did the same again and looked in the next direction. I did it again to look in the next direction.

Finally I saw lighter colored ocean water in a certain direction. That's the way I had to swim. I began to swim in that direction. For each stroke I was moving barely a foot forward with sharp scratches in my legs. Each stroke I had to endure so much pain. It was a struggle of life or death. In order to live I had to continue to swim in the direction of the lighter colored water. There was no other way. There was no shortcut. The moment I quit, it meant death. Each painful stroke was a determination for life. Each painful stroke meant that I was one stroke closer to life. 'I am going to live and not die.' Finally I got out of the seaweed patch to the lighter colored ocean water.

I swam back to the beach where I put my clothes. When I came out of the water I shouted in my heart,

"I am alive! I am alive! I am alive!"

People were doing their usual activities. The world was the same but I was not. To me the world was not the same. I just went through and experienced something that the world does not know. I was between life and death. I went through a life and death struggle and learned what it was like to get my life back. I fought for my life between life and death and learned the way to have my life back while girls my age were playing with dolls at their homes.

It was one time experience but I applied it all my life especially when I was engaged in spiritual battles. Stopping means death. Life is only moving forward inch by inch towards the goal even though every inch is painful. Heavy burden of each prayer means one step closer to victory. Life is not merely living which is given to me. Life is to regain from the life and death struggle. I am a fighter trained in the ocean.

There was another beach beside the one behind the mountain. Another beach was on an island and the beach goers went there back and forth by a passenger boat paying fares. One of my sisters had a summer job working in the locker room. She left earlier to the island with other workers. I left later in the afternoon. I paid my fare and boarded the ship. It was a wooden ship with a motor engine about 50-60 feet long. There were about 30-40 passengers in the ship. The ship left the harbor and headed to the island. I did not know how long it would take to get there but it was about one and a half hours to get there.

The ship came to the open sea. In all four directions there was no island. I was standing beside the side of the ship. Then I noticed a very, very strange sight. There were no waves on the surface of the ocean. The surface of the ocean was smooth like silk, smooth like spilled water. That smooth area was huge as far as I could see and I saw not a single wave on it. And the huge smooth area was spinning just like a top spins. The ship was caught at the edge of the spinning water and couldn't come out of the spinning water even though its motor engine was running. On the other side not far from the ship I could see normal ocean water with waves. I had never seen or heard anything like this.

The ocean was spinning like a top spins. I could not tell the distance of the radius of the spinning circle from where I was standing. It could be tens of miles and miles.The power of spinning was greater than the power of the motor engine of the boat and the boat could not come out of the circle. But what was happening under the ocean water? How incalculable the power was to spin the ocean water on this scale! It was spinning the motor boat as if it spins a piece of wood. I was sure that the captain of the ship and crew members knew about it. But the passengers were not aware of it. They were talking to each other casually. There was no panic in the ship.

I hoped and waited that the ship would free itself out of the spin. I waited for a long time and I began to worry. I began to prepare myself for a possible disaster. The ship might run out of fuel or break down in pieces. There were several rubber tubes tied to each side of the ship for emergency purposes. Strong men would be the first to grab those. I was looking for a piece of wood that I could hold on. I stayed near it. In case I would be the first to grab it. But what if the spiral spinning ocean sucks and swallows everything into it? There would be no chance of survival for anything and anybody. I would call it an ocean black hole.

Eventually the ship freed itself from the spinning and entered the normal ocean water. The captain and the crews did a heroic job at least in my eyes. The ship arrived on the island where there was a beach.

On this island beach I saw a victim of the low tide. On the sandy beach there was a diving board made of wood and fixed on the beach. During high tide the water level rose up to half height of it but during low tide the water level was shallow. A young man dived from the diving board during low tide. He hit his head and people pulled him out of the water. He was lying on the sandy ground. He could not move but was able to answer yes or no to questions. A dozen people stood around him concerned about his injury. I turned around and left the scene. It was heartbreaking to watch it. In the remote island there was no first aid, no doctor, no helicopter rescue, no cell phone. The injured young man had to wait for the arrival of the next ship returning to my hometown.

While swimming, I was like a fish swimming in the ocean. A fish swims basically to look for food but its two eyes also watch vigilantly dangers of unknown, and unseen. I don't enjoy swimming in a swimming pool. Speed is the only concern in swimming pools. There are no unseen and unknown dangers and people can swim in sleepy minds. I have more fun swimming in the ocean than in a swimming pool. I swim in my own nice style but my mind is awake to observe ever changing surroundings vigilantly, diagnose it, interpret it, and make a decision for my safety.

After I left the ocean, I applied my knowledge of what I learned in the ocean to my real life.

To live in the world is not like swimming in a pool but it is like swimming in the ocean. I live my life in my own style but my mind is awake and watches vigilantly the dangers of the unknown and unseen. Otherwise, I may be eaten by a bigger fish.

Chapter 12:
The Only Poem I Read

When my husband turned over in his fifties, he started to show some gray hairs. One day he abruptly said to me; "I could have been an inspired poet. But you killed the inspiration of the poem in me."

I was surprised to hear that from my husband. I felt sorry for him. Did I ruin his promising career as a poet? During our honeymoon, I said to him not to ask me to read his poems. Since then he never showed me his poem. But he kept on writing his poems from time to time and read them alone. He must have felt his poetic inspiration gradually drying up within him. He began to think that it was because of his wife that his poetic ability was drying up. Sure, my rejection to read his poems could have discouraged him and he bore the negative feelings for almost 25 years. But he endured it because he loved me.

I did not say anything to him but mumbled alone to myself; 'I did not tell you to stop writing poems. I just told you to keep your poems for yourself and do not ask me to read them. You should have kept on writing your poems.'

Then he walked to me. "Read this poem." Since I asked him not to bring me his poems, he never brought me his poems for me to read. But that day he asked me to read his poem. "Read this. I wrote about you." He broke my request. I broke my own word, too. I read his poem for the first time.

To My Wife

You always love to be a tree
That blocks glowing rays of summer heat;
And presents cool shade to us.

Never enjoying to decorate your leaves
With seasoning colors,
You love to remain as an evergreen tree.

Alienated from the birth pain,
You went out to the field
To grow new life
In fullness and wisdom of the Lord.

Dreaming the shadowy vision,
I was blind to see the growing buds;
You quietly poured water on them.

You'd stand at the entrance of house
To greet visitors for me
And prepare meals for hungry strangers

Boksoon Kim

Share good things with neighbors
To promote the goodness of the Lord.

Diligence and thrift are your clothes
Gentle smile, your make-up
Sharp intelligence, discretion, your sash

Feminine scent radiates from inner beauty
You are like almond blossom in snow.

Through the storms and sunlight,
Our faith, sublime;
Through laughters and tears
Our love and hope, ascended.

Even when I thought I was parted
And roamed in a strange land,
Your soul flew to my heart from the sky,
Tightly holding my hands, making
Our journey of life, together and whole.

What more words do I need?
In giving the roses of my heart
To the one who loves and loved!

He knew the meaning of each word and I knew what he meant through each word. He compared me to a winter flower which blooms in snow despite all kinds of hardships.

The Half Basement

I knew what he meant that he roamed in a strange land. He was in a land where he had never been before, a land of betrayal, lies, losing everything that he toiled for 13 years from the half basement.

In the strange land, there is no light but only darkness. Yet in the darkness the smiling face Judas Iscariot is seen, every single lie and schemes are vividly remembered and repeated. In a strange land the pleas of a victim does not echo but fades away. A victim falls and is forgotten. My husband was in such a strange land. In the strange land he was lost, thinking about committing a suicide. In the poem he wrote that I held his hand tightly. Yes. I held his hand tightly and never let it go.

Chapter 13:
Good or Evil?

When I left Toledo to settle in Houston I brought one question with me. Why is it that some believers say good as evil, and evil as good? In another word they lost discernment about good and evil.

Humans start to have a sense of good and evil at age around 5 or 6. As humans grow, with the sense of good and evil, they avoid evil and are encouraged to do good. Some people who do not have a discernment of good and evil cause problems in the society and turn out to be criminals.

What is good? What is evil?

Then Jesus asked them, "Which is lawful on the Sabbath: to do good or to do evil, to save life or to kill?" But they remained silent. **Mark 3:4**

We can ask the same question to a 5 or a 6 year old child. Is saving life good or evil? The child can answer. Is killing life good or evil? The child can answer. We can ask any person in the street the same question. Is saving life good or evil? Any person can answer right away without hesitation. Is killing life good or evil? Again one can answer right away. But the religious leaders in the synagogue did not answer, or did not want to answer, or could not answer. Their next action showed what was in their hearts. - Killing Jesus was in their hearts. - Evil was in their hearts.

Then the Pharisees went out and began to plot with the Herodians how they might kill Jesus.

Mark 3:6

They wanted to kill Jesus. Killing life was evil. But they thought killing Jesus was good. They wanted to kill Jesus eagerly. They lost discernment of good and evil. They were not ordinary people. They were religious people. They were servants of God. They dedicated their lives to serve God. They were teaching people about God, to obey God, to love God, and serve God. They study and memorize the words of God all the time. Why then did they lose discernment of good and evil? Why did they think killing innocent Jesus is good?

I saw the same from some believers. They were highly educated elites. They were Bible teachers. They gave their lives to serve Jesus. Why then did they think that they were doing right while they did evil? They thought that they were doing right while they betrayed, lied, deceived, and even signed as false witnesses for fake documents. They lost discernment of right and wrong, good and evil. I considered this as the result of being brainwashed in the religious world.

When I thought about each person one by one, they were highly educated, very good, kind and nice people. They left everything to serve Jesus. What happened to them? What happened to the Pharisees in Jesus' time was also happening in my time, too.

What is the reason? What caused it? What is the root of it?

I had to know and I asked the Lord, "Lord, what made them lose discernment of right and wrong, good and evil?" I don't like to go to the Lord with a question like this. It is not easy on me. I lose appetite and cannot eat well. My mind is squeezed in agony. I have to go through physical and mental sufferings. I have to pray again and again until the Lord answers me and the Lord does not answer quickly. By the time the Lord answers me, I lose 3-4 pounds in weight.

I don't remember how long I prayed for this question, probably several weeks. One day I was on a fishing boat with my husband. The boat was moving from side to side in high waves and I was uncomfortable in the boat. At that moment I heard a voice, saying: "They love praises from men."

This was from John 5:41-44. Jesus pointed out that seeking praise from men was the root problem of the Jews who tried to kill Jesus, who lost discernment of good and evil. Seeking praise from men is the root problem of losing discernment of good and evil, the root of the problem of being brainwashed in the religious world. This was a new world to me because I did not know the connection between seeking praise from men and religious brainwashing.

Praises from a charismatic religious leader are very influential to that religious group. Praises from a charismatic

76

leader can make one a hero of faith, or a villain of faith. Praises from a charismatic leader can make one happy or make one miserable. Members in that religious group gradually seek praise and approval of their charismatic leader. How do they receive praises from their leader? They receive praises by obeying the words of the leader as the words of God. Obeying his word is good, disobeying his word is evil. Eventually those highly educated, wonderful, devoted, nice believers lose their discernment of good and evil.

Jesus said; "I do not accept praise from men." **Mark 6:41**

"How can you believe if you accept praise from one another, yet make no effort to obtain the praise that comes from the only God?" **Mark 6:44**

New young baby Christians are encouraged by words of praises. Baby Christians are motivated by men's praises. But they should not be fixed there. Grown up Christians should be motivated by the praises from God. God's praises come by doing what is written in the Bible. But unfortunately some seek praises from men. Enjoying praises from men eventually leads one to religious brainwashing by losing discernment of good and evil. Jesus did not accept praises from men. Jesus did exactly according to the words of God. Jesus was hated until he was arrested and killed. Do exactly what the Bible says. You will be hated and you will find the way Jesus walked. Why do some people seek praises from men, and some seek praises from God? What is the root of it? Jesus answered;

"But I know you. I know that you do not have the love of God in your hearts." **John 5:42**

People who love themselves seek praises from men through religious activities, and people who love God seek praises from God through their religious activities. It is a problem of love.

Chapter 14:
An Ideal Church

After my husband passed away suddenly, all our family was in shock. My children and I had to go through shock and pain. I had to figure out what I should do, how I should live without him. My children also moved in the right direction. When daddy was with us, they lived where they chose to live. After dad's passing, my children moved back to Houston over a period of several months. My first daughter had her medical internship in Houston. My second daughter managed TaeKwonDo School. My third daughter got a job in Houston and her family moved from Dallas to Houston. My son transferred from the University of Texas in Austin to Rice University in Houston. We were all in close proximity to each other.

When husband and wife had a ministry together, the pastor husband passed away, and the remaining pastor's widow had one of two ways to go; either close the ministry or continue the ministry. I saw both cases in the past and I had to choose one. I decided to continue what we had been doing together.

My husband and I had a campus Bible study with college students once a week. We had been building the Bible study over two years and a dozen students were attending steadily. At home, we had Bible study and Sunday worship service with Korean missionaries. I could not do both. I had to choose one and let the other go.

The campus Bible study can grow faster than the church with Korean missionaries. American students are not shy. Once they receive the words of God, they teach other students very soon.

They love to teach others. Yet they carry problems of sex and drugs. If I choose a ministry of American students, I have to deal with problems of sex and drugs. And I am not good at it. I should not expect loyalty from American students. They stay when the ministry is good for them, but they leave when they don't gain benefits. But that was not my point. I preach the Gospel to any people God sends.

The ministry with Korean missionaries would take a longer time to build up. At least for ten years I should not expect any fruits. It would be a ministry that requires a long wait. It was because our missionaries came from Korea recently. They have to overcome English, culture, visa status, and get a stable job. That preparation would take ten years. They don't have problems of sex and drugs. Though it might take a long time, they are people of loyalty. They do not move by benefits but by their clear goal. They will live with me and die with me.

So which group should I choose? Neither my husband nor I knew Korean missionaries before. When they arrived in Houston, it was the first time we met each other. They came under our wings and I felt I did not want to disappoint them. I wanted to hear from them; "I am glad that I went to missionary James Kim in Houston." For this reason, I chose to continue ministry with Korean missionaries. Someday they would say

"I am glad that I went to missionary James Kim in Houston."
We will bless them, protect them and we want them to have an
abundant life.

'There are thieves who steal from sheep. They throw away
sheep like trash after using them.' Under thieves sheep are still
alive. There are killer wolves who say 'All you have are mine;
your money, your time, your marriage, your wife, and your
children. Sheep lose life under killer wolves.'

"The thief comes only to steal and kill and destroy. I have come
that they may have life, and have it to the full." **John 10:10**

I gave myself about 10 years to build up our Korean
missionaries.

My goals for the next ten years were;

To make a unity of one heart among brothers.

To make each brother as a pastor and a preacher for Sunday
worship service For ten years three brothers and I discussed
every church event in detail and they had been oriented for ten
years on how the church had been served. Each brother had a
chance to deliver a Sunday message once a month. All of them
studied seminary for three years and became ordained pastors.

Then I began to think about what kind of church I would
like to have.

There is no ideal church on earth, ideal church is in heaven. Church is like bread. In order to make bread many ingredients are required. After mixing all the ingredients according to the recipe, bread is baked. The freshly baked bread smells good and tastes good. The good bread does not last long. After several days it starts to be stale and produces fungus. Then people have to throw away the old bread and make a new one.

In the beginning of church, everybody works hard with joy and personal sacrifices. A new ideal church is born. The church grows with success after success. Glory, honor, power, and money fill the church. Then the church begins to corrupt. It is because human minds are corruptible just like baked flour is corruptible. Then next believers come up with a new system correcting the errors of the predecessors. The new system eventually corrupts too. This was what I saw in the 2000 years of the history of churches. There is not a perfect church system in this world. It is because human minds are corruptible.

As a pastor of the church, I began changes. I kept what was good, and changed what was bad.

The first change was from college students centered campus ministry to family centered ministry.

When I was still in Toledo, Ohio, we had to go to a church conference. Children were not allowed to the conference because it was college students centered on campus ministry. My regular babysitter was not available because she was going to go on her vacation. I desperately was searching for a babysitter and I found a family who was a total stranger to my children and me. I left my two daughters with the family and went to the conference.

It took one day to go and one day to return. After the conference, after 6 days, I went to the babysitter's house to pick up my daughters. My first daughter was about 3 years old. She was outside of the house. When she saw me, she ran into the house and did not come out. It broke my heart. Mom put her in a totally stranger's house. She did not know why her mom did that to her. She did not know where her mom went and what her mom was doing. From her side she was abandoned by her mom. It seemed like my daughter had to adopt a new family.

This was wrong. Something was very, very wrong in the church system. I read the Bible to find an answer. In the Garden of Eden God established a family. God made a family as a unit of serving God. God works through a faithful, loving, blessed family. Parents have the responsibility of raising children to keep the way of the Lord.

"For I have chosen him, so that he will direct his children and his household after him to keep the way of the Lord by doing what is right and just…" **Genesis 18:19**

So the ways of God would be handed over from father to his children, from one generation to the next generation. So when my children did not know what their parents were doing, how would serving the Lord be handed over to the next generation? Will they know when they grow older? No. It had been disconnected when they were young, it hurt them when they were young, and it would remain disconnected.

Excluding children for the sake of campus ministry is a short sighted measure. Children grew in the hands of babysitters or grandparents. Mom and dad were always busy with church work. This was wrong. I was told that when I give myself to serve God and have no time to take care of my children, God will take care of them. That was a lie. That was wrong. Children need parents' care and love.

In the Old Testament period visiting the temple to worship God was a family event. The whole family walked to the temple over a week or two weeks and worshiped God together. When little children grew, they did the same to their children, going to the temple to worship God with their children as their fathers did to them. When Jesus was 12 years old, his parents and boy Jesus went to Jerusalem together to celebrate the Passover. It was a family event. **(Luke 2:41,42)**

"Teach them to your children and to their children after them"
Deuteronomy 4:9

"Teach them to your children, talking about them when you sit at home….." **Deuteronomy 11:19**

When I became a pastor of Houston CMI church, I changed our church system to a family centered church, children centered church, a church that is connected to the next generation.

Church retreat was a good opportunity for change.

I welcomed crying babies to the retreat. The crying sounds of babies were our future. When I am too old to serve God, the babies will take my place. I assigned every little child a very simple thing to do for the retreat. Some made a bathroom sign for man and woman by drawing man and woman. Some children were assigned to announce meal time visiting each cabin. Some were assigned to post programs to the wall. They loved to do their assignments. There was Bible study for children during the retreat. They studied the same words of God that their parents studied.

When I am a pastor, children will go to the church retreat with their dad and mom. They do not have to be separated from their parents for 3 or 4 days. They participate in the retreat themselves. They practice songs and dance together with their parents. They know what their parents are doing. Some children love the retreat so much that they pack their luggage two weeks before the retreat. They invite their friends to the retreat.

So did I abandon campus ministry? No. The new system I established was college student ministry based on solid family life, not on broken family life. We raise our children as future Bible teachers. Middle school students whom I taught the Bible to are all now in college.

Another change I made was an elimination of a leader acting like God. It had been practiced that obeying the word of the leader (pastor) is obeying God. This cuts off each believer's vertical relationship with God and leads them to obey humans as if the human leader is God. I was told during Bible study by my Bible teacher that obeying the words of the church leader is serving God. So I did. I served God by obeying the word of the church leader. But as my Bible knowledge increased, I saw that some words of the church leader were not following the teaching of the Bible. So I did not obey and I was told that I was rebellious and proud.

In our church, where I am a pastor, humans would be human, God is God. Each church member should establish a personal relationship with God. Each should take his own problem in prayer to God, and follow a direction given by God.

So there was no supreme leader who acted like God in our church. Instead we had a leader's meeting of three brothers and I. We discussed everything together, and moved on only when all four agreed.

Every family, every person who came to our church were sent by God for me to take care of.

Every family, every person had problems. I felt a heavy responsibility to help them overcome their problems whether it was financial problems, emotional problems, marriage problems, and sin problems. I will divide into three major groups; demon possession, physical sickness, and sin sickness.

The easiest problem to solve was demon possession. It was because I have a lethal weapon against the demons, the name of Jesus. The demon possessed person lived in another state. But I prayed every day in the name of Jesus. After 6 months of prayer I heard that that person improved 90%. I prayed for another 6 months. I heard that that person improved 99%. I prayed for another 6 months. That person was totally freed and serving God wholeheartedly. This healing inspired many who heard about it.

For physical sickness the sick person should see a doctor and receive medical treatment. While receiving medical treatment, they should pray that they may meet the right doctor, right treatment, and right medicine which will lead to healing. Wrong doctor, wrong treatment, wrong medicine may make a sick person even sicker. What medicine and doctor can not heal, the sick must pray to God for healing.

There are incurable diseases. The word 'incurable' is a human word, used by humans, belonging to humans. There is no word of 'incurable' to God. God does not use that word. Everything is possible for the Lord. Everything is possible for him who believes. (Mark 9:23) Nothing is impossible with God. (Luke 1:37) Nothing is impossible for him who believes. God raises the dead to life. Healing the sick and alive is easy for the Lord. It takes a few years or several years to pray for the sick until they are healed. I, myself, was healed from many illnesses, I learned by heart God can heal any sickness.

At work I was doing a dialysis on an old African American woman. She had diabetes which caused her kidney failure. During treatment she kept on cursing diabetes. And she said, "The Lord said to me; I could heal you but you did not ask me for." Through these words I could see the mind of God. He can heal any sickness but the sick believers don't come to the Lord for healing. Instead they accept the sickness, pains, and cursing the sickness.

Yet those who go to the Lord for healing receive the healing. One new person came to our church. She said that she had an incurable disease. Her disease causes her skin to thicken like elephant skin. I said she would be healed. "Give your sickness to Jesus on the cross. We give to Jesus not only our sins but also our sicknesses, too." She said that it was incurable. I said, I gave my rheumatoid arthritis to Jesus on the cross and I was healed. She said it was incurable.

It took months or years. She is totally healthy now and works for the Lord wholeheartedly.

The most difficult group to help was sin-sick people. They enjoy sinning. They love to go back and indulge in their sins. Everybody can see that person's sin except that person. It takes almost 5-10 years to help sin-sick person or family. It is the most difficult group to help. Nothing works to make them repent their sins except the Holy Spirit. It has to be the work of the Holy Spirit to convict the heart of the guilty. (John 16:8) It takes years of persistent prayers. When a person or a family recovers from sins, the whole church sees it and is inspired. The church is being built solidly on the work of the Holy Spirit.

All three groups require the work of the Holy Spirit. When I prayed continuously, I saw the family or the individual's recovery over the years eventually. When a family left our church and moved to another church, I was hurt and felt sorry. Yet I was thankful to them because the burden of prayer for their problems was lifted from my shoulder. Before God, I transferred my responsibility of prayer to the pastor of the church they moved. The pastor in the new church praying for this family or not is not my business.

These fundamental problems should be solved slowly and surely. That's how the church is being built solidly. Without solving these problems of demons, physical illness, and sin problems the church turns to a social group, events centered activity group which may see the end of it when everyone is bored and tired.

After I made these changes the church has been growing for now. It may grow until human hearts bring corruption. Then I hope some godly men may bring reformation.

Chapter 15:

Satan's strategy

Adam concentrated on his job to rule the world God had created. All the beasts of the field and all the birds of the air came to Adam to receive their names. God came and saw how Adam gave each creature its name. (Genesis 2:19,20) And Adam happily married Eve. It was a life in paradise. But life in paradise did not last long.

There was a serpent who was looking at the happy scene of daily life in paradise. The serpent wanted to destroy the happiness of Adam and Eve by separating them from God. The serpent watched the happy couple working for the Lord. The serpent saw the vulnerable spot of the happy life. It was her desire to be as wise as God in her heart.

So the serpent approached the woman and talked about the words of God. After talking with the serpent the woman was in sweet thought of imagining that she would be as wise as God if she ate the forbidden fruit. (Genesis 3:5,6) She ate the forbidden fruit and gave it to her husband by disobeying the command of God.(Genesis 3:6) They were separated from God and expelled from paradise.

The serpent succeeded with one shot. The serpent shot with one shot to the target board and hit the center and finished the job. Adam and Eve were separated from God, lost paradise and lived the remaining physical life away from God.

Is this story just of Adam and Eve? Is this ancient story not relevant today because it was too old? Why then did Jesus teach us in the Lord's prayer that we should pray not to fall into temptation?

"And lead us not into temptation, but deliver us from the evil one." **Matthew 6:13**

Believe it or not the ancient serpent still does the same thing today. The serpent watches Gospel workers, the hard working men and women of God, and gives a shot to separate them from God and destroy them. I received many of these shots but I will share just one.

A healing prayer meeting was scheduled while my husband was still alive. After my husband's passing I did not cancel it. I tried to carry on what he had already planned. Pastor Duksoon Hong from Korea was going to lead the three day meeting. He was gifted with healing ministry and I had heard about healings that had occurred through his ministry.

I prepared the healing prayer meeting on a smaller scale at my house. I invited sick people and healthy people whom I knew who lived in Houston as well as in other cities. The day of the healing prayer meeting came. About 2-3 hours before the meeting, before people began to arrive, I was driving home. About ten blocks away from my house while driving I began to have chest pain. I had chronic chest pain for years and I knew when it was about to start. It starts with a feeling of tying a knot in my heart which soon turns to heavy pressure as if a rock is on my heart. Then I stop everything that I was doing and take deep breaths trying to send more oxygen to my heart. After 4 or 5 minutes I was relieved from the chest pain and I resumed my work. But that day I was driving in the street. As I was driving through the cross road I struggled to avoid a car accident. I was sweating and felt like I was going to pass out. The chest pain got worse. My lower jaw was frozen and locked. Teeth were hurting. Both my shoulders were frozen. I was barely holding the handle of the car. I managed to arrive home. I collapsed on the couch. This was the worst chest pain that I had ever had.

The ancient serpent wanted to destroy the healing prayer meeting. The most vulnerable spot of the whole event was my weak heart. If I fell, the healing prayer meeting would fall apart. The serpent shot with its shot to my weak heart.

I was a nurse of the coronary care unit, specializing in heart problems. Whenever I had abnormal heart beats in my heart, I imagined abnormal EKG rhythms; that's PVC, a big one, that's skipped beat, that's a fib. But that day all the symptoms indicated that I had a major heart attack. I thought that it was my last day. The condition required me to rush to the emergency room right away.

I called my children. I wanted to see their faces before I die. I did not know how much time I had with me before I died. My second daughter arrived first. I gave her my last word to her; Read the Bible. My first daughter arrived from her work. My son arrived from school. My doctor daughter really urged me to go to the emergency room. I answered to her, "No. I must attend the healing prayer meeting." She said, "Mom, you can just see a doctor in the emergency room and come back to attend the prayer meeting." Once I arrived in the emergency room, I would be admitted and lines and tubes would be inserted into my body. I would not be able to come back to attend the prayer meeting.

How about the healing prayer meeting without me? The action of going to the hospital means that I deny the faith of healing by God. Here, sick people gather at my house to receive healing power from God, and my action loudly says I do not trust God's healing power but rather trust hospital treatment. Then all sick people whom I invited should go to the hospital instead of coming to the healing prayer meeting. I'd rather die than to despise healing faith in God. I would not destroy this healing prayer meeting by going to the emergency room. I would stay to keep the prayer meeting to go on even if I might die. There was a conflict between the work of the Holy Spirit and my life. I chose the work of the Holy Spirit over my own life.

My children saw my firm decision and could not do anything. They left. A couple arrived from another state after driving many hours. The doorbell rang. I managed to get up and opened the door. They were surprised to see me saying, "Why are you so pale? Do you have any problems?" I did not say anything. More people began to arrive. Each time I got up and greeted them at the door. My friend who was dying came leaning on her cane. I was gradually gaining strength and did my duty as a host. And the healing prayer meeting started.

When God allowed Satan to test Job, God allowed Stan to do everything, except Job's life.

"Very well, then, everything he has is in your hands, but on the man himself do not lay a finger." **Job 1:12**

My life is in God's hand. If the Lord decides that it is time for me to go, then no matter what I do, I would die. If the Lord says it is not the time for me to die, then no one is allowed to touch my life. The serpent hit my heart and made me feel almost dead, but I did not die because my time had not come yet.

Because of my determination to protect the healing prayer meeting even to death, Satan failed to destroy the prayer meeting. The healing prayer meeting continued Friday, Saturday, and Sunday. Saturday night they prayed loudly to the Lord. They put their hands on sick people and prayed for the sick one by one. I heard miracles of healing from pastor Hong's healing ministry but no miracle happened. Every sick person returned home without healing.

After this,
A week passed.
Two weeks passed.
Three weeks passed.

Then I realized I did not have any chest pain. I was free from chest pain that I had for more than 15 years. Even when I was sleeping, I woke up from sleep because of chest pain. Rolling side to side in my bed I had an agony feeling a heavy rock on my chest. But for three weeks I did not have any chest pain!!! It was a wonderful new life to live without chest pain. I felt so peaceful and comfortable to live my daily life. I was the only one who received healing from this healing prayer meeting.

I was free from chest pain for 6 years from that time on and after 6 years I began to have chest pain again. With the recurrence I went to a cardiologist and had thorough tests for heart; EKG, Echocardiogram, and heart catheterization. There was some minor abnormality in echocardiogram, but the rest were negatives. The cardiologist said to me; "Don't come to see me anymore."

Even though I had symptoms of a major heart attack, I knew it was Satan's shot trying to destroy the healing prayer meeting. Satan's shot often came right before the work of the Holy Spirit. Whenever I prepared a church retreat, I had to guard my mind too and be ready for the coming of the one shot from the ancient serpent. If I fell, the whole retreat would crumble down.

After retirement I was no longer the target board of the ancient serpent. But the pastor who succeeded me, will see the activity of the ancient serpent right before a major church event.

Chapter 16:
From Crystal Beach To Allen Camp

Our church was planning a retreat. The place would be at a beach house in Crystal beach just like the year before. There were many oceanfront or ocean view beach houses for rent through the rental office. We wanted a big beach house which can accommodate about 30 people. The estimated rent for two nights and three days was about $3,000. I received a check of $1,500 from our church to make a down payment for the rent.

Crystal beach is in Bolivar peninsula. In order to go to the Crystal beach from Houston, we first drive to Galveston Island. The Bolivar peninsula is 2.7 miles away from the north tip of Galveston. Instead of building a bridge of 2.7 miles over ocean water, ferry boats carry cars and people back and forth all day long.

In Galveston Island, we follow a sign 'to ferry ride' and we arrive at a wide parking area waiting for the next ferry boat. Ferry boat comes every 30 minutes but when there are many cars, we have to wait for the next ferry which means over one hour of waiting. When the ferry arrives, attendants guide each car where to go on board and where to park on the ferry. Once I counted the number of cars on one ferry and it was over 70 cars. I stopped counting because I realized it was useless to count. Big cars like buses, cars with trailers took spaces for 3-4 smaller cars. Once the ferry is fully loaded with cars, the gate is closed and the ferry moves for next 20 minutes sailing over the ocean. All these are free.

Once the ferry moves we come out of our cars. Some go to the front, others go to the back, others to the sides, and others to the second floor for a better ocean view. There are plenty of pelicans sitting or flying. A group of white seagulls are flying to follow the back of the ferry. I did not see anyone feeding the seagulls but I heard that the seagulls follow the ferry to catch fish propelled to the surface of water by the enormous propeller of the ferry. Besides, it is not uncommon to see dolphins passing in groups. I saw them several times.

20 minutes pass very quickly. All people return to their cars. The ferry arrives at the southern tip of the Bolivia peninsula. Again the attendants guide each car when and which way to leave. All cars exit one way and on the opposite side a couple of hundred cars are waiting at a parking lot to go to Galveston and to Houston.

The day I decided to go to the rental office at Crystal beach, I invited two women who were from another state visiting our church family. Visiting Galveston Island and ferry ride would be an exciting experience to them. I drove to Galveston with them. I parked and we walked along the long Galveston beach watching pelicans, seagulls, and the blue ocean.

Then I was thinking. 'Next we have to wait for the ferry and cross the ocean. Then drive to the rental office and visit the rented house. Come back to the ferry to go back to Galveston. This will take at least three hours. They would be too tired.' - I did not want them to feel hungry and tired. I decided to do just one thing. I would focus on serving them only and I would come back to the rental office next time. So instead of crossing the ocean on a ferry, we went to a restaurant for lunch.

After a couple of days I decided to go to the rental office. I asked one church mom whether she wanted to go with me. She was under stress and I thought that she may feel better if she saw the ocean instead of staying in her apartment all day long. She was free except she had to pick her son from school when the school was over. I calculated the time and I said to her that we would return before she picked up her son. So we left together.

We arrived in Galveston, crossed the ocean by ferry, and arrived at the Bolivar peninsula. Crossing the ocean took more time than I thought. The rental office was within 10 minutes driving. Then I had to think. Should I drive 10 minutes to the rental office and spend another 10 minutes to sign the contract and drive back another 10 minutes? After that I will have to park and wait for the ferry. That meant that she could not pick up her son on time. I told her about the situation. She said that she could call her son to wait for her because she would be late.

I consider keeping promises very important. I'd rather keep my promise to her that she would return to be able to pick up her son. She also had a promise with her son to pick him up after school at 3pm. If I go down to the rental office, two promises would be broken; my promise to her, and her promise to her son. So I decided to keep two promises and not to go to the rental office. I turned the car around and parked for the ferry waiting to return to Houston.

I arrived home. I was thinking. I went to Galveston twice to make a rental contract. I was even ten minutes away from the rental office. Why couldn't I make a contract? Of course I had a reason each time. But, is the Lord telling me something? Is the Lord telling me not to make a contract? Is the Lord blocking the way? Is the Lord telling me to find somewhere else?

I often pray to know the Lord's guidance; open the way if that is the way I should go and block the way that I shouldn't go. The decision was made through the church leader's meeting and the way was blocked twice. We rely on our experiences and seek the best for the church. But we do not know tomorrow, we do not know the future.

I opened my computer and typed 'retreat center in Texas.' The word 'Allen camp' showed. I read the information. It was one hour driving from my house. Right away I drove to Allen camp. One woman showed me around the camp. The camp had amazing scenery around a lake. There was a fishing deck and several canoes. A group of ducks were moving on the lake peacefully. I made a reservation for three lake side cabins and paid half of the price for the reservation. The total price was just half of the beach house rent. Usually reservation was made a year in advance but luckily the cabins were available for us. Travel time was also just one hour from Houston. It was amazing to see how the Lord knew a better place for us.

Our church made every decision in the leaders' meeting which consisted of three brothers and I. This process would delay another week or two to get approval. In this case I signed the contract, secured the retreat place, and I decided to get approval later. We can have our retreat at a closer site, and with half price and in a better facility. I reported to the church what I did and we will have our retreat not at a beach house but at a new place called Allen camp. Some expressed they would miss a beach house.

Exactly two weeks later, the Houston area was embracing a huge hurricane. We prepared emergency supplies for ourselves. All eyes of the Houstonians were on TV news to see which direction the hurricane would pass and hit. When I saw on TV the picture of the totally destroyed Crystal beach, I was awestruck. The hurricane hit the Bolivar peninsula and wiped all the beach houses at Crystal beach. Not a single beach house remained.

Just two weeks ago, I was there trying to make a rental contract. I did not know a hurricane was coming. The Lord knew that the beach would be totally destroyed in two weeks. That was the difference between God and a human.

An elementary school boy said that God led Pastor Kim to move the church retreat from the Crystal beach to Allen camp because God knew that the destructive storm was on the way. He was an elementary school boy but he had eyes to see what the Lord was doing. But not everybody saw what the Lord did.

"Blessed are the eyes that see what you see." **Luke 10:23**

Chapter 17:
Two Different Systems

I invited a middle aged Korean woman to our Sunday worship service. She asked what the name of the pastor was. I answered, "We don't have a pastor." She asked again, "Who then preaches on Sunday?" I said," I do." At this, her expression on her face turned weird, and shook her head. She might have seen two things we were doing that were not allowed in her church system. First, only ordained pastors can preach on Sunday. Second, unordained women are not allowed to preach for Sunday worship services. Both points were correct in her church system.

According to her belief in the church system we should not have even Sunday worship services at my apartment. I should not preach because I was not ordained and I was a woman.

Since then I did not invite Koreans to our worship services any more. I invited non Koreans, Americans. American students did not question my credentials. They listened to my message and they came again to listen to the words of God.

I came abroad alone with desires to serve God. I had just the Bible with me and no knowledge of the church system. I only knew that the words of the Bible are alive, active, and have the power to save sinners when sinners listen to the words. I came to preach the words. That led me to many Bible students, Bible studies, and eventually to start Sunday worship services and to preach. Am I wrong? Have I done wrong things against some church system? I did not do these alone. God led me to the half basement. God taught me how to prepare Sunday sermons. God gave me strength to go on. God showed in Young's dream that college students' ministry was coming.

If I was doing wrong things, God would have stopped me. But He did not. The number of Bible students increased and they surrendered their lives to serve God.

The Korean woman did not know that her knowledge of the church system was not the only system to serve God. There was another system to serve God which is just following what the Bible says. I did not know the church system. I did not need the church system. I was not under the church system. I did and followed what the Bible says. That is the system I was under. I could do whatever the Bible says.

I was 65 years old when I finished my seminary studies and was ordained as a pastor. I was fully qualified to preach. But I did not wait until I was qualified. I started to preach the words when I was 22 years old because that was what the Bible says. I put my time, energy, money, youth, and zeal to preach the words for the next 40 years. What could I do at age 65 if I had waited until I met all the requirements under the church system? I have seen such people. They had a desire to preach. After they worked to support their families, they finished seminary studies, and were ordained as pastors in their 50's or 60's. They did not have many years to serve in their old ages.

I preferred the system I was under. And I am thankful that I could jump in my young age instead of waiting and preparing till I have gray hairs to be qualified. I am glad that the Lord sent me abroad only with the Bible and allowed me to work freely following the words of God.

Preaching is men's turf. Only recently women have been ordained and allowed to preach.

When a male preacher messes up with his preaching, the audience graciously tolerates. But a female preacher messes up with her preaching, the audience does not tolerate it. So I put ten times more effort than men do when I prepared a message.

Even so, there are people who do not approve of women's preaching. Their favorite words are

"Women should remain silent in the churches. They are not allowed to speak, but must be in submission, as the Law says. If they want to inquire about something, they should ask their own husbands at home; for it is disgraceful for a woman to speak in the church." **1 Corinthians 14:34, 35**

During the second mission journey apostle Paul went to Corinth and taught the words of God for a year and a half. (Acts 18:11) Then he left Corinth. After Apostle Paul left, what might the Corinthian believers have done without Apostle Paul? The men in the church of Corinth worked very hard after Apostle Paul's departure. The proof was that the church of Corinth grew after Apostle Paul's departure. To the church of Corinth

Apostle Paul gave the words 14:34, 35. Brothers worked hard to build the church and women supported them quietly in submission and prayers. That was the best way to do the work of God.

But when men do not preach, and do not work as hard as the men in the church of Corinth, do these words still apply? In my opinion when men do not preach, women should preach. When men do not teach the Bible, women should teach the Bible. Men who are busy with computer games, sports, movies, hobbies, and do not preach, they must not criticize women who preach by quoting the words of 1 Corinthians 14:34,35. Men do not preach, and women do not preach, then what might happen to the churches? Churches would have to shut their doors which is happening in Europe.

Koreans men are busy with mandatory military service, studying, and getting jobs to establish family life. So I do not blame them for not preaching the words of God. But the words of God should be preached by someone else. So I preached the words. Any man who has not taught, does not teach the words of God, please, do not quote the words of 1 Corinthians 14:34, 35 to silence women Bible teachers and preachers. But ask yourself; Are Christian men teaching the words of God diligently so that women may stay silent in prayers?

Chapter 18:
A Door That Opens

I was in Seattle and just finished a week of seminary studies. Three months ago it was prearranged that I would give the Sunday sermon that weekend at the Seattle Good Shepherd church. Saturday night I could not sleep because of worries. While everyone was sleeping I came down to the basement of the pastor Joshua Lee's house where I was staying. I did not know what time it was because usually I did not have a wrist watch. I came down the stairs to the basement in the darkness very quietly so as not to disturb others' sleeping.

For our seminary studies professors from the International Seminary in Seoul came to Seattle and gave lectures for seminary students for one week. Then they returned back to Korea. This time there was a graduation ceremony and ordination ceremony after the usual one week seminary studies. So the CEO of the seminary school and the dean of the graduates department also came along with the professors who gave lectures. They did not return to Korea after the ceremonies but stayed for Sunday worship service at the Seattle Good Shepherd church.

I found out just the night before that I would preach that Sunday morning before 6 seminary professors including the

CEO of the seminary school and the dean of the graduate school.

This was not what I expected. I was overwhelmed by their presence. Just thinking about their presence made my mind shrink. What if they close their minds because I am a woman? What if they despise my preaching? What if they laugh at my message in their hearts? What would the professor of preaching think about my message? They were experts in this field with lots of experience. It would be very hard to inspire them.

I regretted that I promised to give Sunday sermon that day. But how could I know that the professors would attend the Sunday worship service three months ago? Had I known that, I would have never, never wanted to give the Sunday message. I rebuked myself. 'You invited this stress into your life yourself. From now on, just go home after finishing your business. Don't try to show up yourself." I rebuked myself and instructed for future direction through this disaster. Still that was not a solution. I still had to give a Sunday message that morning before the church congregation and 6 seminary professors.

I became so sad. I thought about my pains which I buried deep in my heart after my husband's death. But this time I let it loose out of my mind. After my husband's death I decided to continue the church he was serving. I took over Bible studies and Sunday sermons. During Bible study I ran to the bathroom. I poured my tears into the bathroom sink, washed my face, put on my eye glasses to cover my swollen red eyes and returned to continue Bible study. This was a sad story of a pastor's widow. Remembering this made me feel even worse. I went as far as I could go but then I could not go any further. I was defeated, desperate and helpless. I was at the end of my rope. There was no solution and the time was ticking every second closer to Sunday worship service.

Out of desperation and misery I asked Jesus, "Lord, I am so miserable now. Please, hug me." Soon Jesus hugged me with His arm. I did not see His arm but I felt the strength of hugging. He did not hug me with two arms, but one arm of Jesus embraced my right side for a few seconds. I felt heavenly. Jesus' love and peace spread through my body, heart, and soul. I remained happy for a while. All my sorrow, pain, fear disappeared. People in hopeless situations tend to turn to other people. That's the wrong direction. Turn to Jesus.

Jesus is not a legendary figure written in the Bible. He is real. He died and was raised from the dead. He is alive. He hugged me and I was fully recharged in my body, heart, and soul by His love. When all my human efforts and strength failed, Jesus recharged me with His love. It took only a few minutes. I rose with the love and power of God from a pathetic weeping widow. I rose as a mighty woman of God in a matter of a few minutes. David described this in Psalm 23:2 "He restores my soul." Jesus just restored my soul.

I was filled with love, power, and spirit. I got up from the chair. I did not have much time left for the Sunday worship service. I must use this remaining time strategically. Let's go to work! I went outside.

The best strategy with a short time is prayers that invite God's help. I must invite God's power through prayers. I must use the remaining time to maximize prayer support from others for my message as much as I can. I did not think anyone would remember that I would deliver the Sunday message that morning and pray for me. Rather, they would think about what they would eat for breakfast. I must initiate prayer support. I must ask them to pray for me. I must make them pray for me.

I walked to the church. There was one person whom I did not know cleaning the church floor. It did not matter whether they knew me or not. I walked to him and said, "I am going to give the Sunday message for the worship service this morning. Would you pray for me?" He said, yes. He and I prayed briefly for my message and the Sunday worship service for about 3-4 minutes. After the prayer a woman just arrived probably for morning prayers. I did not know her either. I walked to her and asked the same. She said, yes. She and I prayed together for my message and the Sunday worship service for a few minutes. I waited for the next person to arrive. I moved on to the next person, the next person, the next person…

It was close to the time for the worship service. All the church members and seminary professors were seated. I looked around and approached one last person, the CEO of the seminary school. I asked him the same and he agreed to pray for me. So the CEO and I prayed together. And the Sunday worship service began. Of course I skipped breakfast. As I was trying to have prayer support as much as I could, there was no time for eating.

When I stood before the lectern to preach, I was confident without any fear. I usually deliver my message standing at one spot behind a lectern and follow the written manuscript. But that day I walked out from behind the lectern, abandoning the written manuscript. I walked back and forth using the whole space, even saying something instantly that was not written in the manuscript. I just felt the presence of the Holy Spirit, and the Spirit's moving inside of me and among the audience and the entire place. The passage was Mark 5:21-43 about resurrection faith. The message was the best message I had ever preached in my life.

After the Sunday worship service, one professor came to me and said, "You are very bold. You went to the CEO and prayed with him. We don't dare go near him. We don't dare talk to him." Just two hours ago I felt the same way. The presence of the CEO made me shrunken. But after I received the love and power of Jesus, I stood before him to proclaim a message of resurrection faith to him. He was also a human who needed a message of resurrection. Indeed I was bold to proclaim resurrection faith to everyone in the worship service.

After lunch I went to bed very early. I stayed up most of the night and I did not eat breakfast. So I was exhausted and could not stay up. While I was sleeping, the professor of preaching visited me to see me. But since I was sleeping, he returned without seeing me. I really respect that professor and I missed hearing his comment on my message.

Several days ago, I talked to pastor Joshua Lee on the phone. He said that a while ago he talked to a person who did not know me, but attended the Sunday worship service when I preached. He heard my message and wondered how such a powerful message came out of me. It was almost ten years ago but he still mentioned my message.

There is a door that does not open and there is a door that opens. A door does not open because there is no one behind the door. When there is no one inside, the door will not open no matter how long, how hard one knocks on the door. But there is a door that opens. The door opens because there is someone inside. God is behind the door of God and God opens the door. As long as God exists, the door opens.

"Knock and the door will be opened to you." **Matthew 7:7**

"To him who knocks, the door will be opened." **Matthew 7:8**

A door of failure: A person who is successful in the world does not come to the door of despair. A totally failed person arrives to the door of despair. All four directions around, up above and down below are closed with no way to turn. Then he comes to the door of despair. When he knocks on the door of despair calling God, the door of despair turns to a door of God.

A door of God: The world of flesh is over, he knocks on the door of a new world, a world of God. Knock, knock, knock, bang, bang, bang…until it opens. The door of God opens to a different world, to the spiritual world, to the world of God, Almighty. Once the door opens to him, he is destined to be successful because he knows a new world where nothing is impossible and everything is possible.

Many stand in front of the door of total failure. But many do not find the door of God. It is because they stop knocking after a few hours or after a few days. They turn back to the world where they failed and turn to a survival mode. Why did he go back to the world where he failed? He must not stop but knock until it opens to him.

I want to ask people who failed and do not want to live anymore. Can you bang, bang, bang, knock, knock, and knock on the door of God until it opens? There is no requirement to knock on the door; no money, no policy, no baptismal certificate, no religion, no experiences. It is just between God and a desperate human. The door is designed to open for you and you will see a new world.

I was there before the door of despair as the most miserable creature in the basement of Pastor Joshua Lee' house. In my distress I knocked on the door of God, "Please, hug me." The door of God opened to me and I was flooded with heavenly love.

It was amazing how the Lord Jesus changed my disaster into a victory. I was elated by this miracle. The next day I flew back to Houston. That weekend I delivered the same message during Houston CMI worship service. I expected the same excitement that I saw in the church in Seattle a week ago.

I delivered exactly the same manuscript and I did not change a single word. But the audience remained cold. They did not respond to the message. What's going on? Why didn't they respond to my powerful message? The manuscript was the same, the speaker was the same. One was different. In the church in Seattle, I prayed with as many people as possible and the Holy Spirit came. In Houston CMI church I did not pray. I was not desperate and I did not knock on the door and the Holy Spirit did not come. I saw the differences with prayer and without prayer.

Made in the USA
Columbia, SC
01 July 2024

37798115R00063